Work

THE ART OF LIVING SERIES
Series Editor: Mark Vernon

From Plato to Bertrand Russell philosophers have engaged wide audiences on matters of life and death. *The Art of Living* series aims to open up philosophy's riches to a wider public once again. Taking its lead from the concerns of the ancient Greek philosophers, the series asks the question "How should we live?". Authors draw on their own personal reflections to write philosophy that seeks to enrich, stimulate and challenge the reader's thoughts about their own life. In a world where people are searching for new insights and sources of meaning, *The Art of Living* series showcases the value of philosophy and reveals it as a great untapped resource for our age.

Published
Clothes   *John Harvey*
Deception   *Ziyad Marar*
Fame   *Mark Rowlands*
Hunger   *Raymond Tallis*
Illness   *Havi Carel*
Pets   *Erica Fudge*
Sport   *Colin McGinn*
Wellbeing   *Mark Vernon*
Work   *Lars Svendsen*

Forthcoming
Death   *Todd May*
Middle Age   *Chris Hamilton*
Sex   *Seiriol Morgan*

Work

Lars Svendsen

ACUMEN

For my parents

First published in 2008 by Acumen

Acumen Publishing Limited
Stocksfield Hall
Stocksfield
NE43 7TN
www.acumenpublishing.co.uk

ISBN: 978-1-84465-154-2

British Library Cataloguing-in-Publication Data
A catalogue record for this book is available
from the British Library.

Designed and typeset by Kate Williams, Swansea.
Printed and bound by Biddles Ltd, King's Lynn.

Contents

Introduction   1

1. From curse to vocation: a brief history of the
   philosophy of work   13

2. Work and meaning   29

3. The distribution of work   49

4. Work and leisure   57

5. Being managed   73

6. Getting paid   87

7. Work in an age of affluence   97

8. The end of work?   111

9. Life and work   119

   Further reading   129
   References   131
   Index   136

Introduction

In 1954, when my father was fourteen years old, he became a plumber's apprentice at a shipyard in Moss, a small industrial town in the southeast of Norway. The shipyard primarily built large tankers. It was the largest company in Moss, and 2,000 workers were employed there. At the age of eighteen my father became a regular plumber, and about ten years later he became a foreman. In 2002 he retired owing to health problems, having been exposed to large amounts of asbestos at the shipyard early in his career. He was employed at the same company for his entire professional life. My impression was always that he, for the most part, enjoyed working at the shipyard. Yet he was also eager to leave at exactly 3.30pm every single workday, and as a child I usually met him at the gates of the shipyard before we walked home together. There was a very strict distinction between work and leisure, and my father had limited contact with his work colleagues outside the workplace. If a particularly close colleague had fallen ill, he might pay him a visit in the afternoon, but otherwise work and leisure were strictly isolated social spheres. Questions as to whether his job was "meaningful" or whether it was an expression of his "true self" do not seem to have occurred to him.

This description of my father's career is in many ways the exact opposite of current descriptions of what work is supposed to be all about. The current ideology of work is that it should be meaningful and entertaining, that one's colleagues should be one's friends and that work is primarily a tool for self-realization. Furthermore, with the development of new technology, work has become deregulated in terms of where and for how long it takes place, thereby blurring the distinction between work and leisure. We change jobs at an increasingly higher rate. Few now have a job for life, and radical changes of career in the middle of one's working life are more and more common. And even though we live longer than before, we spend fewer years at work.

I have the sort of job that seems to be all about self-realization, as to a great extent I can spend every workday exactly as I like, but I nevertheless frequently wonder: is my work really meaningful? Is this what I am supposed to do with my life? At least once a month I consider leaving the university to find something more worthwhile to do. The difference between the attitudes to work of my father's generation and mine seems to be so great that one is tempted to say that we live in different worlds, but I also think that my father and I share a lot in our experiences of work. Even though my father never reflected much on work and identity, his work at the ship-yard was clearly a significant part of who he understood himself to be and how he was regarded by others. Without that job, he would have been deprived of an important source of meaning in his life. The same holds for my job as a philosopher. We both take our jobs seriously; there is certainly pride involved. Even though neither of us are particularly religious, we are both Protestants in terms of our work ethic. And without work we would probably both go mad. (Since his retirement my father has brought my mother to the verge of insanity, since he is incapable of relaxing for more than a few minutes at a time, and has redecorated every room in the house several times.) The idea of a world without work would probably fill us both with despair.

But imagine a world without work. It would differ significantly from the world in which we live, but it is far from obvious that it would be a *better* world. In a world without work, we would no longer have our jobs as essential markers of our identities. Social relationships would have to be formed on a new basis. We would lose some – or maybe most – of our sense of purpose in life. We would have more time to spend, but on what? Our entire lives would have to be re-imagined. Some argue that "the end of work" is drawing near, that a world without work is our historical destiny. While I don't share that view, such a world nevertheless supplies an interesting thought experiment, as it brings out how great a role work actually plays in our lives.

This book will focus more on the existential than on the political aspects of work. The *meaning* of work will be my major concern. Of course, I would not dream of thinking that a strict or "analytical" distinction could be made between the existential and the political aspects of work, since work and politics have been intertwined for as long as there has been work and politics. It is a question of emphasis. Issues of gender, social class, ethnicity, disability, migration, and globalization will not be addressed to any great extent. I shall draw on various philosophical, historical and sociological sources but with the general reader as my target. Also, my focus will be on Western societies; to cover the working conditions of people in the developing world would be an altogether different essay.

Some people may ask what a philosopher might possibly know about work. After all, doing philosophy does not seem like "real work", does it? I can certainly see their point. I guess that most people who become full-time philosophers do so out of some sense of vocation: the feeling that this is what they are *meant* to do in life. Others may regard doing philosophy full time more as a permanent vacation than as a vocation. Reading some books, lying on a couch thinking, writing a few pages and saying something supposedly "profound" is not much of a job, is it? If any readers wonder if I have ever had anything resembling a "real job", eight years of part-time work as a cleaner might count. However, I confess that I do not follow John Locke's recommendation that every scholar should spend three hours a day on manual labour, because one also needs to exercise the body and not only the mind.

Much academic writing on work does seem to be carried out at such a distance from its object that it actually loses its connection to it, and it becomes more or less irrelevant except as a part of the academic industry itself. This danger is perhaps especially great for philosophers. All genuine philosophy begins with experience, and in this sense philosophy is reflection on an experience or a meaning that is already there. Philosophy therefore gets its content and legitimacy from something pre-philosophically given, and I believe that it must retain its relation to this if it is to maintain its legitimacy. The problem with so much academic philosophy is that we tend to get lost in abstractions and lose sight of the experiences that made us philosophize in the first place.

If we are to understand the role of work in our lives today, we must also look at what work has meant for earlier generations. We need the past in order to make sense of the present. If we go back a century, workers had no overtime pay, no paid holidays, no health insurance, no pension, no job security and no unemployment benefits. They worked significantly longer hours, and would probably have characterized today's work as "part-time". I will not argue that work today is perfect – on the contrary, I believe that a thorough-going ambivalence to work is hard to avoid – but compared to what it was in earlier days, we should be fairly contented today. It is therefore strange that so many people believe that work life in general has worsened. According to a study from the Pew Research Center (2006), Americans believe that workers today have to work harder for less money, with fewer benefits and less job security than a generation ago. Are they correct? If we compare real wages, working hours and unemployment a generation ago with today's numbers, there seems to be little foundation for such pessimism. Job security may be lower in many countries, but still most of those who leave an employer do so because they choose to, not because they lose their job.

This negative attitude towards today's work life can be seen as a part of the very notion of work. The etymological roots of the various words for work in different languages indicate that it is something highly unpleasant. This is especially clear in the case of the French *travail*, which stems from the Latin *tripalium*, which was an instrument of torture composed of three sticks. The Greek *ponos* means sorrow, the Latin *labor* refers to drudgery and the German *Arbeit* meant hardship and adversity. The Hebrew *avodah* has the same etymological root as *eved*, which means "slave". Modern dictionaries are not quite as negative. If we consult one it will typically give us keywords such as "a job", "involves physical or mental effort", "to manage something to gain benefit from it", "to use a particular material to produce an item" and so on. These can be quite different activities; for instance, we can have a job without using a material to produce an item, and many jobs are "unproductive" in that sense. We can also "work out", which means to exercise. We can even "work something off", that is, get rid of an uncomfortable feeling or thought, by "working out". There are other meanings to the word "work", but the meaning we shall stay closest to in this book is "job". However, the term "job" is not unequivocal either. Two of the main meanings of "job" are "paid work" and "a particular task or piece of work that one has to do". It doesn't seem possible to define "job" without using the term it was supposed to explain, namely "work". It is therefore of relatively little help.

The *Concise Oxford English Dictionary* claims that work is "expenditure of energy, striving, application of effort or exertion to a purpose". Yet, we certainly would not consider everything that requires effort as work. Playing tennis is physically exhausting, but very few people would argue that playing tennis constitutes work. As the scientist Robert Boyle pointed out in the 1640s: "Tennis, which our gallants make a recreation, is much more toilsome than what many others make their work; and yet those delight in the one and these detest the other, because we do this out of necessity, and the other out of choice" (quoted in Thomas 1999: 9). As a teenager, I played a lot of tennis, as much as three to four hours every day in the summer, constantly trying to improve my game and become more successful in tournaments. However, hard training can only compensate so much for a lack of natural talent for the game, and at the age of seventeen I quit after realizing that I had reached my peak, and that my peak was well below the level of the best players in the country. I took tennis very seriously then and, except for writing my doctoral dissertation, I have never put as much effort into anything as I did in tennis. No matter how much effort I put into it, nobody would call what I did "work" in a proper sense of the word. The amount of effort involved does not seem to be essential for whether or not something should be described as work. A different criterion is clearly needed. My brother was much more talented than me, and he was among the top players in the country. For a while he considered becoming a full-time player in order to try to make it as a professional. He eventually chose to get an education instead, and that was probably a wise choice, but had he become a full-time player, his playing tennis could then have been described as "work", especially if it had provided him with a decent income. He would then have stopped being an amateur, that is, someone who does something only for the *amare* (love) of it.

The economist Alfred Marshall suggested that work is "any exertion of mind or body undergone partly or wholly with a view to some good other than the pleasure derived directly from the work" (Marshall [1890] 1907: 65). This definition clearly does not suffice either, since a large number of activities that we would usually not see as work would satisfy it, for example, taking a long walk simply because one likes to do so would not be work, but as soon as some other motive is present, such as getting into shape, the activity would immediately be transformed into work.

Perhaps money is the essential characteristic that decides whether or not something should be considered "work". That does not seem to be the case either. Were the years my mother spent at home looking after my brother and myself "leisure", whereas her years as an accountant for the social services were "proper work"? I assume that my mother would disagree. A more extreme example is slavery, although some would argue that housework is tantamount to slavery. Slaves do not get paid, but it would be unreasonable to argue that consequently they are not working. A large part of all the work that has been done throughout history – from the pyramid builders of ancient Egypt to the Africans working in the American cotton fields – has been done by unpaid slaves. Including money in the definition does not therefore help to give us a satisfactory definition of "work" either.

Mostly, we intuitively grasp what constitutes work and what does not. And then we do not appear to need a definition. I am reminded of the verdict in the obscenity trial, Jacobellis v. Ohio (1964), where Justice Potter Stewart stated: "I shall not today attempt further to define the kinds of material I understand to be embraced within that shorthand description; and perhaps I could never succeed in intelligibly doing so. But I know it when I see it." We usually know what is work and what is not when we see it. However, it can sometimes be difficult to draw the line between work and non-work, and to decide on which side of the line a given activity should be placed. For example, is begging work? George Orwell, unlike most people, argued that it is. In *Down and Out in Paris and London*, he writes:

> Beggars do not work, it is said; but, then, what is work? A navvy works by swinging a pick. An accountant works by adding up figures. A beggar works by standing out of doors in all weathers and getting varicose veins, chronic bronchitis, etc. It is a trade like any other; quite useless, of course – but, then, many reputable trades are quite useless. ... A beggar, looked at realistically, is simply a businessman, getting his living, like other businessmen, in the way that comes to hand. He has not, more than most modern people, sold his honour;

> he has merely made the mistake of choosing a trade at which
> it is impossible to grow rich. ([1933] 1972: 173)

I think Orwell is correct. We would be hard pressed to give a definition of work that excludes begging but includes all the other activities we tend to categorize as "work".

In my own case, I must admit that my job is often such that I
am reluctant to categorize it as "work", even though I get paid to do
it. I frequently choose to stay at home for a couple of days, rather
than go to my office at the university, and I can lie on the couch in
my living room with my cats on my lap, sipping coffee and smoking
cigarettes while I read a book that I find so interesting and entertaining that I would have read it in my spare time anyway. Aristotle
would not have recognized what I was doing as work; rather, he
would have seen it as leisure. It is only fairly recently in human
history, with the emergence of professional academics, that what I
do would be characterized as work.

At certain times, the distinction between work and non-work has
been relatively clear, as when a worker would sell his or her labour
to a factory owner for a specific period of time and spend that time
at the factory. There used to be a fairly sharp distinction between
work and leisure, the time owned by employers and the workers'
own time. This was closely linked to a separation of the work space
and the private space. Work could then be defined in terms of time
and place. Of course, this is still what work is like for a large number
of workers, probably the majority, but new patterns of work have
also emerged, where the worker is neither in a specific place every
day – he or she may spend some days in the office, others at home –
nor works a specified number of hours. This is particularly the case
for the growing category of "knowledge workers". For these people,
it can be relatively difficult to specify exactly when they are at work
and when they are not. The emergence of new technologies such
as the mobile phone and the internet has had a big impact on these

distinctions. One can say that with this new flexibility, the very distinction between work and non-work has become blurred both in terms of time and space. Flexitime is more and more common, and people have more individually tailored schedules than before. What we could call "flexispace" has also gained ground, where it no longer matters where we do the work as long as we do it. For many people the office is no longer a particular room in a specific building, but rather the equipment they carry around: the laptop computer and the mobile phone.

Work can be paid or unpaid, entertaining or boring, liberating or akin to slavery. Work is a curse to some and a blessing to others, and a little bit of both to most of us. In *The Conquest of Happiness*, Bertrand Russell points out: "There are in work all grades, from mere relief of tedium up to the profoundest delights, according to the nature of the work and the abilities of the worker" ([1930] 1996: 162). Work can be a radically different experience for different people. General statements about work being such and such therefore tend to be misleading because work can be, and has always been, so many different things. Work is like this for some people and like that for others, depending on who they are and what sort of work they do.

Work is one of the most universal features of human life. Virtually everybody does it. As Karl Marx wrote: "The labour process is the everlasting nature-imposed condition of human existence" (Marx 1867: 290). Very few people manage to avoid work. Even those who are wealthy enough to not have to work usually do so. This universality can also be rather misleading, since work is also such a diverse phenomenon. A Norwegian philosophy professor, an American CEO and a Columbian coffee farmer all work, but the differences between their experiences of work are probably more numerous than the similarities. Any statement about work "in general", should therefore be treated with some caution. On the other hand, one must use such broad generalizations and simplifications if one is to get any sort of grip on the phenomenon.

At the most basic level work is about changing the external world such that one can get the necessities of life. We work in order to survive. This simple model applies far more directly to agricultural societies than to modern societies. As human history has evolved, the relation between work and survival has become looser and looser. There is a world of difference between the immediate rela- tion people in agricultural societies had to the food and clothes they had created themselves and the relation a computer programmer has to these things today. If the computer programmer were to consume only the things that he himself produces, he would be very cold and hungry. There is still a relation between production and consumption for the computer programmer, but it is more indirect: mediated through the institution of money.

There is another side to work, where it is not only about bringing about external goods such as food, clothing and shelter – or a car or flat-screen television – but also about bringing about internal goods, such as fun and personal development. Some even argue that only through work can we become who we are, that is, realize our human potential. We do not only create something outside of ourselves in work, but also create our own identity. We learn a lot about ourselves in an activity that occupies so many of our waking hours for so many years: about our abilities, our relations to others, and our role in the social fabric. Work has been the central axis around which we organize our entire life plan. There is no escaping the question of work when we are thinking about what we are going to do with our life. Or about what we have made out of it.

Work seems to be essential to our idea of identity. When we read someone's obituary, work is usually prominent in the description of their life. When we meet people for the first time we usually ask them what they *do*, meaning what they do for a living, as if that gives us instant access to what sort of people they are. If we meet someone at a party and hear that he or she is a psychologist, cashier, musician, fire-fighter or investment banker, our perception of that person will inevitably be shaped by their profession. In the television comedy *Seinfeld*, the character George Costanza, who has a less than impressive professional life, repeatedly lies to strangers and tells them that he has far more interesting jobs than he actually has. He claims to be an architect or a marine biologist just to come across as a more interesting person. When his lies are exposed, he looks even more pathetic. It is nevertheless clear that we do make an inference from what someone does for a living to what kind of person he or she is. Such inferences will often be mistaken, but there is some foundation for making them. What we do day in day out will necessarily influence our entire attitude to the world and to ourselves. Nobody can simply leave their working self at work and not to some extent bring it with them to the other parts of their life. Of course, not everyone identifies with one's job to an equal degree. For some people it is their main source of identity, whereas others' identities are based more on their relations to friends, family or a hobby.

Philosophers and social scientists have often been so occupied with describing the miseries of work that the satisfactions work can bring are left out of the picture. It would be hard to imagine a job that has no "internal goods", that is, a job that brings no rewards other than money. Of course, all jobs do not have equal amount of goods. A job where we can pursue our main interests, be among people whose company we enjoy and feel that we make a small contribution to making the world a better place clearly contains more internal goods than a job where none of these are the case. It simply would not be true to say that "a job is a job is a job".

The fact that work is such an enormously varied phenomenon, with so many aspects, prevents any simple answer to the question "What is work?". There is no single truth about work, but a multitude of truths, depending on who we are, what we do, how we do it and why we do it. This book does not set out to present and defend a "thesis" about work. It is more of a collection of snapshots of various aspects of work, of what it has been, of what it is and

11

what it perhaps will become. I do not seek to present the reader with answers to how they should relate to work. Given the diversity of work, not to mention human diversity, any allegedly universal answer would be pretty misleading. I settle instead for the more modest aim of offering some perspectives and suggestions. Ludwig Wittgenstein wrote: "Work on philosophy is … actually more of a work on oneself. On one's own conception. On the way one sees things. (And what one demands of them.)" (Wittgenstein 1998: 12). I believe that he was correct. Such self-reflection cannot be "outsourced". One has to do it for oneself. What I hope this book will do is help the reader see a few more things that might have been overlooked and to think a few thoughts that might have remained unthought.

1. From curse to vocation: a brief history of the philosophy of work

When one looks at the history of ideas, two main perspectives on work stand out: some see work as a meaningless curse and others see it as a meaningful vocation. The first view dominated from antiquity to the Reformation, and the second from the Reformation onwards.

There has probably never been anybody who has held work in lower esteem than the classical Greek philosophers. There is no separate word for work in ancient Greek, just as there is no separate word for what we call art. The Greeks used different terms for different productive activities. The Greek word that is often translated as "work", *ponos*, primarily refers to strenuous, but not necessarily productive, actions. As with the concept of art, we deal with this lack of a single term for work by projecting our current concept back on to Greek culture, while at the same time trying to avoid too many anachronisms.

Although the standard assumption is that no culture has detested work more than the ancient Greeks, the real picture is a little more complicated. The poet Hesiod regarded work as hard, but also believed that it was through work that one would be blessed by the gods. In *Works and Days*, written in the seventh century BCE, he writes:

Gods and men disapproves of that man who lives without working, like in temper to the blunt-tailed drones who wear away the toil of the bees, eating it in idleness. You should embrace work-tasks in their due order, so that your granaries may be full of substance in its season. It is from work that men are rich in flocks and wealthy, and a working man is much dearer to the immortals. Work is no reproach, but not working is a reproach; and if you work, it will readily come about that a workshy man will envy you as you become wealthy.

(Hesiod 1999: 46)

The moral in *Work and Days* is that labour is man's inescapable lot, but that those who are willing to work hard will acquire wealth and live a good life. Hesiod also makes clear that man's life would be far better if he did not have to work: if he lived in the Golden Age when earth produced food in abundance and work was simply superfluous. That age, however, is gone, so there is no real alternative to work.

From this description of work in *Work and Days* we can see that the Greeks had a far more nuanced conception of work than is commonly believed today. The crucial distinction for the Greeks was between necessary and voluntary activities, not between productive and non-productive activities. It was not work as such that was demeaning, but only a certain kind of work: that which was performed out of necessity. When we look, for instance, at the heroes in Homer's two epics, the *Iliad* and the *Odyssey*, we find them engaged in all sorts of productive activities, as when Achilles carves up meat and Odysseus builds a house and a ship; he even makes his own bed. There is no indication that these productive activities in any way diminished their heroic status, and the reason is that they voluntarily chose to do them. If they had wanted to, they could just have told somebody else to do them. Since they could have chosen not to do any of these tasks, doing each of them was a free act that was an end in itself. This is the crucial difference between their acts and those of the ordinary craftsman or manual labourer. The point is that the ordinary worker would be demeaned because he had to produce something out of necessity – in order to provide a livelihood – whereas an aristocrat could produce exactly the same object simply because he liked to, and not be demeaned by that activity because it was voluntary. Whether or not a particular task would be considered demeaning depended on the social status of the person performing the task.

Those who had to work were considered to be inferior. What was considered demeaning was therefore the social position of the person forced to work to provide the material necessities of life; the activity in itself was considered to be quite all right. Hence, if a nobleman decided to make a chair, he was not demeaned by that activity, since he was free to do what he liked, whereas the carpenter was demeaned because he was forced to produce the chair from economic necessity. The carpenter would also be subject to the wishes of the customer, and was therefore lacking in autonomy. Any man who was not free from the will of others was also regarded as not free in political debate, and it was therefore thought that he should be denied political influence. It is important to see that the very activity of producing something was not in itself demeaning, and what mattered was the social status of the producer. But with Plato and Aristotle, the activity of work itself became demeaning, and even corrupted the soul.

The Greeks began to classify various sorts of work depending on how much of a toll they took on the human body, and those that involved the most physical strain were usually regarded as the most despicable. Aristotle argued that these activities were the most "slave-like" (*Politics* 1258b35). He admitted that a craftsman possessed knowledge but for him it was restricted to a specific area of expertise. The craftsman did not develop his intellectual capacities such that he would be able to grasp the true essence of virtue (1337b). Therefore the craftsman could not become a proper citizen of the state, and the same went for farmers; for some reason, however, Aristotle was willing to consider making an exception for painters and shepherds (1258b35, 1330a26).

What made manual labour and commerce so demeaning? In the case of manual labour, it was not simply the fact that it involved physical activity. The Greek philosophers were generally positive about physical exercise and sports. Indeed, Plato was a wrestler; his birth name was Aristocles, but we know him by the nickname meaning "broad" or "broad-shouldered" given to him by his wrestling instructor.

So what was so problematic about manual labour? In effect, the manual labourer, the *banausos*, was regarded as little different from a slave. Plato makes a strict distinction between the manual labourer and the philosopher, and argues that only the latter is free (*Republic* 495, 590). Furthermore, while sports and leisure make the body and mind fit for military and political purposes, manual labour wears them both down, rendering them useless. Plato's views are, in fact, not quite this clear-cut; he criticizes the wealthy who live a life of leisure and argues that they should regard the carpenter as a role model and then argues that students of philosophy should love all forms of labour, even manual labour (405–8, 535d).

It is nevertheless Plato's rejection of manual labour that has become the conventional presentation of his views. This view is presented even more clearly by Socrates' contemporary Xenophon in his dialogue *Oeconomicus*, in which Socrates says:

> In fact, the so-called "banausic" occupations are both denounced and, quite rightly, held in very low esteem by states. For they utterly ruin the bodies of those who work at them and those of their supervisors, by forcing them to lead a sedentary life and to stay indoors, and some of them even to spend the whole day by the fire. When their bodies become effeminate, their souls too become much weaker. Furthermore, the so-called "banausic" occupations leave a man no spare time to be

concerned about his friends and city. Consequently such men seem to treat their friends badly and to defend their countries badly too. In fact, in some cities, especially in those reputed to excel in war, none of the citizens is permitted to work at the banausic occupations. (1994: 121–2)

In his *Politics*, Aristotle uses *banausos* as a derogatory term, meaning "cramped in body" and "vulgar in taste" (1341a7, 1337b7). He compares the slave and the manual labourer and argues that not only the slaves, but also all other workers, are "enslaved" by the will of others. Aristotle argued that just as the purpose of war is peace, the goal of work is leisure (1333a). Work can never be anything other than a means to an end for those unfortunate souls who are not wealthy enough to escape this dreadful curse. According to Aristotle, work stood in the way of the realization of human potential because it took time and energy away from the development of virtues, which was the true goal of human existence.

Work was a hindrance to the proper use and development of reason. Given how little Plato and Aristotle thought of manual labour, one could believe that they would think more highly of commerce, which does not take such a toll on the body. One could hardly be more wrong. Plato places merchants at the bottom of his hierarchy in the *Republic*. They are people driven by their appetite rather than reason, and Plato makes it perfectly clear that the republic would be heading for a disaster if such people were to have any political influence. In the *Laws* his derision goes even further, and he writes that commerce makes people scheming and unreliable, which in turn leads citizens to become unfriendly and untrusting towards one another (*Laws* 705a). He therefore makes it a crime for the citizens of the state to make their living from commerce; that sort of activity will have to be done by foreigners, and they must be closely monitored, since merchants are notorious crooks (915–20).

17

Aristotle also makes it patently clear that merchants should have no political influence (*Politics* 1328b35). The merchant is a person who makes his livelihood from false values, and even makes the crucial mistake of regarding profit as an end in itself (1256ff.). One can hardly get further away from Aristotle's vision of the good life. The whole point of human existence, as Aristotle sees it, is to reach happiness, which is the same as "living well" (*Nicomachean Ethics* Bk 1). Happiness and living well are identical. The only thing that is an end in itself is happiness, and everything else is a means to this end. Aristotle argues that the merchant confuses profit, which can never be more than a means, with the end. He thereby lives a very one-dimensional life and fails to develop most of his human qualities; Aristotle would say that the merchant is vulgar and stupid because he is incapable of reasoning well about the things that contribute to living well.

The views of the Greek philosophers have often been taken as representative of the status of work in ancient Greece, but this is not necessarily the case. On the contrary, craftsmen seem to have taken great pride in their work, and a number of epitaphs exist in which they boast about their skills. What is more, there were competitions among craftsmen, in which the winner received a crown. A large number of sculptures, pottery and plaques depicting craftsmen at work also seem to indicate that the philosophers' views of work were not necessarily widely shared. The views of Plato and Aristotle have nevertheless usually been regarded as the "official" view of work in ancient Greece.

With the emergence of Christian culture in the Middle Ages, the philosophy of work was transformed. In Christian thought, work as we know it is a result of the expulsion of Adam and Eve from the Garden of Eden. There was no work motivated by necessity in Eden; Adam and Eve could simply stretch out their hands and eat fruits from the trees. But one fruit was forbidden, and eating it led to severe punishment: banishment from Eden. From that point on, humans were subjected to the burden of work: "By the sweat of your brow you will eat your food until you return to the ground" (Genesis 3:19). Work was still regarded as a curse in the Middle Ages, but it was also a *duty*. The idea of work as a duty was inconceivable for the Greek philosophers, but Christian ideals introduced a completely new perspective. The fourth-century Church Father Augustine condemned idleness and encouraged the monks of Carthage to engage in manual labour. The sixth-century founder of monasticism Benedict's view of labour is that it functions as penance: it is a punishment for the flesh. It also keeps us from being idle, and idleness is regarded as harmful: "Idleness is the enemy of the soul. Therefore, the brothers should have specified periods for manual labour as well as for prayerful reading" (Benedict 1998: 47). According to the thirteenth-century philosopher and theologian Thomas Aquinas, all humans have a duty to work in order to improve themselves, help others and pay respect to God. This is the first step towards what would later become the Protestant work ethic. Work still played a subordinate role in the relation to God, where prayer and meditation were far more essential, and it was still regarded as lacking any intrinsic value.

This changed dramatically with the Reformation, which developed a view of work as something positive for all people, even the wealthy, and radically expanded the idea of a *vocation*. The notion of a vocation or calling was well known prior to this, as monks and clerics followed their vocation by devoting themselves wholeheartedly to God and withdrawing from the mundane affairs of society in general. For the sixteenth-century monk and church reformer Martin Luther, the best way to serve God was to devote oneself to one's profession. This is the essence of the idea of a *vocation* or *calling*. What God required was not only prayer and the occasional good deed towards one's neighbours, but also a life that as a whole consisted of work and worship. Luther took the monastic ideal of a life devoted as a whole to God, moved it outside the walls of the monastery and transformed it into a universal work ethic. What is more, the "mundane" jobs were regarded as at least as praise-worthy as those of the monks in secluded monasteries: "The works of monks and priests, be they never so holy and arduous, differ no whit in the sight of God from the works of the rustic toiling in the field or the woman going about her household tasks" (Luther [1520] 1915: §3.42). All jobs became a part of God's great plan, and doing your job as well as you possibly could was a religious duty. You should also stay in the profession you were born into, as God had given you this profession and placed you in the social hier-archy; being a "social climber" would simply be rebellion against God's authority.

One might say that the Protestant work ethic is the exact oppo-site of the Greek idea of work. Work is regarded as having a value beyond that of providing life's necessities. The Protestant regarded work so highly that all things not associated with work – especially those that are enjoyable and give pleasure – were taken to be of a more dubious nature. One should take pride in one's work and do it as well as possible. There is also an idea of justice here, in that hard work would be rewarded and that success is an indication of having served God properly.

The sixteenth-century Protestant reformer John Calvin devel-oped Luther's ideas further, and claimed that everybody should work, even the rich, because it was God's will. Contrary to the traditional suspicion against money in Christian thought, Calvin argued that one had a religious duty to choose the profession that would bring the greatest income. It is strange that Protestantism should become the main force in the spread of capitalism, particu-larly since Christianity had been characterized by a strong aversion to money. After all, in the First Epistle to Timothy St Paul writes: "For the love of money is a root of all kinds of evil: which while some coveted after, they have erred from the faith, and pierced themselves through with many sorrows" (1 Timothy 6:10). And the

Gospel of Matthew says: "No one can serve two masters, for either he will hate the one and love the other; or else he will be devoted to one and despise the other. You can't serve both God and Mammon" (Matthew 6:24; cf. Luke 16:13). Calvin managed to circumvent this, and make the accumulation of money rather a true sign of being a faithful servant of God. This was a significant transformation. As we saw earlier, Luther believed that trying to climb the social ladder – or change career – would be a rebellion against God's authority. Calvin, on the other hand, argues that one should choose the profession that would pay the most at any one time. You could change your vocation at any time. This was an idea that would be important for workers' liberation, and the gradual emergence of workers' rights to sell their labour to whomever they would like made this more common.

This work ethic, as described by the sociologist Max Weber in *The Protestant Ethic and the Spirit of Capitalism*, sounds pretty miserable, since a central feature is "a strict avoidance of all uninhibited enjoyment" (Weber [1905] 2002: 12). It is an ascetic ethic in which the accumulation of wealth is not intended for consumption. As Weber puts it, the hard-working Protestant gets nothing out of his wealth "for his own person, except the irrational sense of 'fulfilling his vocation'" (*ibid.*: 24). He regards the Protestant as irrational because there is not reward for the hard work. Earthly possessions do not really matter to the Protestant, who aims much higher: for heavenly salvation. This salvation is predestined for the lucky chosen ones, and there is nothing – no good deeds or intentions – that could affect the ultimate outcome for the individual. One's destiny is already determined, no matter whether one chooses to live a life of virtue or of vice.

The question is why the Protestant puts in all the hard work when it has absolutely no effect on the ultimate outcome. Weber argues that the Protestant does not work in order to change his destiny, since he is fully aware of the impossibility of doing that, but rather in order to comfort himself, as success in the realm of work can be regarded as a sign of grace. Calvin argues that those who have been saved will put their hearts and souls completely into trying to fulfil God's wishes. Such zeal would in itself make no difference to the chance of salvation, but God would have willed that the chosen ones were model citizens, so if you act as a model citizen, this can be taken as a sign that you are in fact among the chosen ones. The Protestant lives a life full of existential anguish, and success at work could indicate that one fits into God's great plan, and that one is therefore a likely candidate for salvation. If one was to be a fully functioning part of God's great plan, much more than the occasional good deed would be required: one would have to make one's entire life into an integrated whole of good work.

After a while, the theological foundations of the Protestant work ethic started to fade away, but the ethic itself remained. Perhaps the most famous representative of this secularized ethic was Benjamin Franklin, who argued passionately that wealth was a result of virtuous actions. Franklin did not leave God completely out of the picture, but work was no longer primarily conceived of as a form of worship. The worker now fundamentally had his own interests at heart, but in working hard to acquire wealth he would also indirectly serve God, who in turn would reward him. As Franklin put it, "God helps those who help themselves" (Franklin 1987: 1201, 1296) (People sometimes believe that this is a quotation from the Bible, but it could be argued that the Bible teaches the exact opposite – that God helps the helpless [Isaiah 25:4].) In order to achieve success in life, one should display the following thirteen virtues: temperance, silence, order, resolution, frugality, industry, sincerity, justice, moderation, cleanliness, tranquillity, chastity and humility (Franklin 1987: 1384ff.).

This work ethic seems to have lost much of its force. Fewer and fewer people seem to believe that hard work as such is particularly ennobling. However, the Protestant heritage still has an impact on our relation to work. In fact, overall employment is 6 per cent higher in countries with a predominantly Protestant population than in countries in which other religious beliefs dominate.

The nineteenth-century Scottish writer Thomas Carlyle took this idea of work as a blessing to its extremes. One might even say that, rather than founding a work ethic based on religion, Carlyle made work itself into a religion:

> For there is a perennial nobleness, and even sacredness, in Work. Were he never so benighted, forgetful of his high calling, there is always hope in a man that actually and earnestly works: in Idleness alone is there perpetual despair. Work, never so Mammonish, mean, is in communication with Nature; the real desire to get Work done will itself lead one more and more to truth, to Nature's appointments and regulations, which are truth. (Carlyle [1843] 1965: 196)

In effect, Carlyle describes what we today call a workaholic. The workaholic uses work as an escape from all the difficulties in life, fully immersing himself in it such that he no longer thinks of anything else that might bother him. Carlyle writes:

> Consider how, even in the meanest sorts of Labour, the whole soul of a man is composed into a kind of real harmony, the instant he sets himself to work! Doubt, Desire, Sorrow, Remorse, Indignation, Despair itself, all these like helldogs lie beleaguering the soul of the poor dayworker, as of every man: but he bends himself with free valour against his task, and all these are stilled, all these shrink murmuring far off into their caves. (*Ibid.*)

Idleness becomes the ultimate vice, no matter who the culprit is, and Carlyle is just as harsh in condemnation of the idle rich as of the idle poor. He reduces Calvinism to a single element: the work ethic. He lifts the idea of work to such noble heights that none of the grit of real work remains. Even though Carlyle was living at the height of the Industrial Revolution, his idealistic view of work was not affected by his almost equally strong condemnation of the effects of current technology on humanity, which he argued had made humans "mechanical". Is work – in itself – necessarily ennobling? As a general truth, that is hardly the case. To take an extreme example, are prisoners in labour camps "ennobled" by the work they do? No, it is demeaning and breaks them down. There is a world of difference between the prisoners in such camps and the worker who finds true, personal meaning in what he or she does. Whether and to what extent work has the qualities Carlyle ascribed to it depends on what kind of work one does and how one relates to it. The philosopher John Stuart Mill, Carlyle's contemporary, had a scathing reply to Carlyle's praise of work:

> Work, I imagine, is not a good in itself. There is nothing laudable in work for work's sake. To work voluntarily for a worthy object is laudable; but what constitutes a worthy object? On this matter, the oracle of which your contributor [Carlyle] is the prophet has never yet been prevailed on to declare itself. He revolves in an eternal circle round the idea of work, as if turning up the earth, or driving a shuttle or a quill, were ends in themselves, and the ends of human existence. Yet, even in the case of the most sublime service to humanity, it is not because it is work that it is worthy; the worth lies in the service itself, and in the will to render it – the noble feelings of which it is the fruit; and if the nobleness of will is proved by other evidence than work, as for instance by danger or sacrifice, there is the same worthiness. While we talk only of work, and not of its object, we are far from the root of the matter; or, if it may be called the root, it is a root without flower or fruit.　　　　　　　　　　　　　　　　　　　　([1850] 1984: 90–91)

Mill was hardly the only one to argue against such a philosophy of work, and many others were to come, such as Marx's son-in-law, Paul Lafargue, who in *The Right To Be Lazy* ([1883] 1999) dismissed the "strange delusion" of the love of work and said that one should dispel the "sacred halo" that had been cast over work. However, Mill is particularly interesting here, as he was a striking example of what we might call the Romantic transformation of work.

For the Romantic, what it all comes down to is *meaning*. And not any kind of meaning, but a personal and individual meaning that should fill the meaning-void created by the absence of God. The Romantic does not know what exactly he is looking for, except that it should be some sort of infinite meaning and one that has to be realized by the individual. Calvin's idea that everyone should choose the profession that would pay the most, and that one could change one's vocation at any time, was transformed into an idea that everyone should aim for the work that would give them the most meaning and satisfaction. Such meaning no longer had any relation to God, but only to the individual who was supposed to realize his or her individual potential to the fullest.

Today we have in many ways inverted the Protestant ethic. Hedonism has replaced ascetics – to a far greater extent than Mill would have approved of – and gratification shall now be instant rather than delayed. Is there anything left of the idea of work as vocation? We can safely say that for most people, work serves no transcendent purpose. Of course, this was the problem with the Protestant work ethic from the beginning. For most jobs, the alleged relation between the work one did and the religious dimension was not perceptible in the work itself. This relation was straightforward for the monk working in the monastery, but the religious relevance of farming, carpentry or work in a factory was not as easily seen. Very few people seem to think that their work is a religious duty, but some aspects of this idea remain, such as the notion that hard work is an indication of one's moral character.

We can see traces of the idea of "work as vocation" in today's search for one's "true self" at work. We change jobs at an increasing rate. The idea of vocation has been transformed by modern individualism. We are no longer serving God, but rather ourselves, and our primary obligation to ourselves as "individuals" is to realize ourselves. Hence, work falls under the general heading of "self-realization", and to a great extent becomes a question of choosing a "lifestyle".

We are extremely concerned with finding the *right* job. We think that there should be a fit between the job and the person doing it. The idea is that a job can be right or wrong for you, depending on what sort of person you are. To some extent this was discussed by Plato and Aristotle, but, writing 2,000 years before the emergence of modern individualism, they considered it in rather different terms and did not frame it in terms of the unique individual, but rather in terms of what class or general kind different people belong to. We frame it differently in terms of every single individual having their own true vocation, which consists in becoming who they are meant to be as allegedly unique individuals.

Each and every one of us is supposed to be someone *special* these days – or at least to appear to be. So much has changed since William H. Whyte's 1956 study of office life, *The Organization Man*, in which a CEO has the following advice to young executives: one should be "an individualist privately and a conformist publicly" (1956: 156). This no longer holds, as now we must appear to be non-conformist, to go against the grain, in public. Individualism is so pervasive these days that it is hard to think of anything more conformist. If you emphasize your own individuality, you definitely do not go "against the grain", since everybody does that these days. This paradox was made brilliantly clear in *Monty Python's Life of Brian*, when Brian stands on a balcony and addresses the crowd:

Brian: Look, you've got it all wrong! You don't NEED to follow
ME, you don't NEED to follow ANYBODY! You've got to think
for yourselves! You're ALL individuals!
The Crowd (*in unison*): Yes! We're all individuals!
Brian: You're all different!
The Crowd (*in unison*): Yes, we ARE all different!

(Chapman *et al.* 2001)

Perhaps the most unnerving expression of this ideology is a song, "I am Special" (to the tune of "Frère Jacques"), which is apparently being taught to American children:

I am special,
I am special,
Look at me,
You will see,
Someone very special,
Someone very special,
It is me,
It is me.

The emergence of individualism gave the individual a new responsibility for himself and a duty *to become himself.* We are all Romantics, and we are therefore firm believers in a notion of self-discovery, where it is a question not of finding an already given self, but of making one up. An authentic self is one that is self-fashioned. Work becomes a tool in this process of self-fashioning.

We can call this a Romantic transformation of the idea of the vocation. The problem with being a Romantic is that you are never really satisfied – at least not for long – as you never fully achieve that ultimate, personal meaning you aim for. When work fails to satisfy our Romantic desire for meaning, it fails as a vocation and rather looks like the sort of curse the ancient Greeks took it to be. Work then appears to stand in the way of your personal development. So you have to move on, either to a new company or up the corporate ladder, facing new challenges, believing that this new job will bring you greater satisfaction. And you manage to think so for a while. It is described well in Joshua Ferris's novel *Then We Came to the End*:

> How we hated our coffee mugs! Our mouse pads, our desk clocks, our daily calendars, the contents of our desk drawers. Even the photos of our love ones taped to computer monitors for uplift and support turned into cloying reminders of time served. But when we got a new office, a bigger office, and we brought everything with us into the new office, how we loved everything all over again, and thought hard about where to place things, and looked with satisfaction at the end of the day how well our old things looked in this new, improved, important space.

The satisfaction will not, of course, last for very long.

2. Work and meaning

Olav, a friend of mine, worked for the post office in order to pay his bills while he was studying. His job was to turn mailbags inside-out in order to see if any letters were stuck in the bags. One day, while turning yet another mailbag inside-out, the utter futility of human existence struck him, and he started sobbing like a child, although, being a good Protestant, he kept on doing his job as the tears ran down his cheeks. The problem was that he saw no end to what he was doing; there would always be another mailbag coming in. There seemed to be no progress, just the eternal recurrence of the same.

Olav's situation at work was in some respects similar to that of Sisyphus. According to the Greek myth, Sisyphus was condemned by the gods to roll a rock up to the top of a mountain, only to have the rock roll back down to the bottom when he reached the top. And then he would start rolling the rock back up, before it rolled down again. In *The Myth of Sisyphus* (1942), Albert Camus argues that the gods were wise in understanding that an eternity of futile labour is the most dreadful of punishments: "The gods had condemned Sisyphus to ceaselessly rolling a rock to the top of a mountain, whence the stone would fall back of its own weight. They had thought with some reason that there is no more dreadful punishment than futile and hopeless labour" (Camus [1942] 1991: 119). However, Camus ends his essay by stating, "One must imagine Sisyphus happy" (*ibid.*: 123). Must we? I find that hard to fathom.

We must be able to see some *point* to what we are doing. One can say that Olav's minor breakdown was in fact caused by his own lack of imagination. If he had thought about how the letters he found in the mailbags could affect people's lives, it would probably have been far more bearable. He could have thought about how one letter perhaps was from a son who had been estranged from his father, trying to piece their relationship back together, how another was perhaps a love letter to a soldier stationed abroad and how yet another could be a letter of admission to a university somebody had dreamt of going to. Olav could have thought so, but he did not. All he could see was an endless row of mailbags.

Immanuel Kant claims that humans are the only animals with an existential need for work (Kant [1803] 1902– : 471). Without work, we would simply be bored to death because work provides our lives with *content*. He argues that amusements cannot fill this function in the long run, and that a person who fills his or her life only with amusements will feel increasingly "lifeless" ([1798] 1902– : 271). Action, not pleasures, is what we need: "If a man has done much, he is more contented after his labours than if he had done nothing whatever; for by work he has set his powers in motion" (2001: 154) Kant seems to overlook a crucial point: not all work is meaningful! Much of it is excruciatingly boring.

More than 33 per cent of the 10,000 workers surveyed in a large American study from 2005 claimed that they had too little to do at work and that they were understimulated (Malachowski 2005). That number is well above the number in most studies of workers who claim to suffer from stress. It is therefore not unlikely that boredom is a bigger problem than stress in the workplace today. In the cartoon series *The Simpsons*, Homer is always trying to get through his days at the nuclear plant doing as little as possible; his ideal workday contains no real work whatsoever. But how many of us would actually endure doing virtually nothing day in and day out, year after year? However, boredom is not a burden only on those days when we have virtually nothing to do; there is also the boredom of the heavy workload. Boredom is a question not of having too little or too much to do, but of managing to find *meaning* in what one does. When we do not manage to find such meaning, time becomes a terrible burden. In Ferris's *Then We Came to the End*, the narrator writes:

> Some days felt longer than other days. Some days felt like two whole days. Unfortunately those days were never weekend days. Our Saturdays and Sundays passed in half the time of a normal workday. In other words, some weeks it felt like we worked ten days straight and only had one day off.

These people work, but they hardly manage to find the sort of meaning that work supposedly contains.

The existential need Kant attempts to grasp is therefore not one for work as such, but rather for meaning. Work can be meaningful, but it can also be the opposite. One can even say that only something that can be meaningful can also be truly meaningless. The need for meaning is a fundamental human need, and work is one of the primary sources of such meaning. Work without meaning, on the other hand, can be akin to torture. In *The House of the Dead*, Fyodor Dostoyevsky writes:

> The thought once occurred to me that if one wanted to crush and destroy a man entirely, to mete out to him the most terrible punishment, one at which the most fearsome murderer would tremble, shrinking from it in advance, all one would have to do would be to make him do work that was completely and utterly devoid of usefulness and meaning.

Some jobs have a greater potential for meaning than others and the conditions under which one works have a strong impact on whether or not meaning is provided. This is the problem Marx attempted to address with his theory of alienation (Marx

[1844] 1994: 71–96). The Latin term *alienation* had previously been used to describe the phenomenon of becoming a stranger to other people, one's country or God, and to refer to insanity and being deprived of one's property. The specific meaning of Marx's concept of alienation is hard to pin down, and it seems to contain aspects of all the various meanings of the Latin term and a few more in addition. It is therefore a concept that resists a straightforward definition. Alienation can only affect a being with a certain potential. As Marx sees it, alienation is a state in which this potential is not being properly realized. The question, of course, is what this potential is supposed to be. It is clear that Marx perceives it as something that is supposed to be realized through work, because it is in work that man expresses his essence. Marx distinguishes "objectification" and "alienation", and argues that only a being with a need for objectification can be alienated. When humans work and transform the external world, they objectify themselves in external goods. According to Marx, this is essential for the realization of human subjectivity: we create something external that is also an incarnation of our own subjectivity. In work human beings reshape the outer world, and thereby create an external manifestation of themselves. Humans can then recognize themselves in the world that they have created. In alienated labour, this fails to happen. Alienation can be described as objectification led astray by the forces of capitalism. Marx criticizes capitalism for putting the worker in a situation in which he is not "at home" in the world as a worker. In the state of alienation the work is in some sense external to the worker, or at odds with his or her humanity. We cannot address all aspects of Marx's theory of alienation, so let us narrow it down to one feature he took to be essential: the division of labour. His general idea is that the division of labour leads to a fragmentation of the creative process, with endless repetitions of minute operations, which in turn makes work meaningless.

Plato discussed the principle of division of labour, but for him this meant that each worker would dedicate himself to a particular craft, depending on his natural talents. In the modern factory system this principle has been taken to a completely new level, in which the division is no longer between crafts, but rather between specific tasks. If one should highlight one feature of modern work that makes it stand out from what work used to be earlier in history, it would probably have to be this increasingly radical implementation of the principle of division of labour. The philosopher and economist Adam Smith was probably the first to grasp the consequences of this. In significant ways Smith's theory of the division of labour is the opposite of Plato's. Smith was a strict egalitarian, and Plato was not. For Smith the division of labour creates the difference between people; it is not a consequence of differences in their natural talents. As a consequence, these divisions are not given once and for all in accordance with nature, but are constantly evolving such that the divisions will differ in traditional and modern societies. Smith was clearly correct here. In traditional societies, there are usually only twenty to thirty different occupations, whereas in modern societies there are several thousands, perhaps as many as 30,000.

At first Smith's presentation of the division of labour appears to be positive because he emphasizes how the division of labour has been the most important factor in the improvement of productivity. In the first part of *The Wealth of Nations*, he describes work in a pin-factory:

One man draws out the wire, another straightens it, a third cuts it, a fourth points it, a fifth grinds it at the top for receiving the head: to make the head requires two or three distinct operations to put it on, is a peculiar business, to whiten the pins another; it is even a trade by itself to put them into paper; and the important business of making a pin is, in this manner, divided into about eighteen distinct operations, which, in some manufactories, are all performed by distinct hands, though in others the same man will sometimes perform two or three of them.   (Smith [1776] 1981: 15)

He goes on to explain how this makes possible a vast increase in the number of pins one can produce in a day compared to how many would have been produced if each worker had worked independently and made complete pins. It is also fairly obvious that such work will not be personally fulfilling. On the contrary, I believe that some of us would prefer a gunshot to the head over having to work in that pin factory; it simply does not strike one as work fit for human beings. Smith himself clearly also recognized this.

In the progress of the division of labour, the employment of the far greater part of those who live by labour, that is, the great body of the people, comes to be confined to a "few very" simple operations; frequently to one or two. But the understandings of the greater part of men are necessarily formed by their ordinary employments. The man whose whole life is spent in performing a few simple operations, of which the effects too are, perhaps, always the same, or very nearly the same, has no occasion to exert his understanding, or to exercise his invention in finding out expedients for removing difficulties which never occur. He naturally loses, therefore, the habit of such exertion, and generally becomes as stupid and ignorant as it is possible for a human creature to become. The torpor of his mind renders him, not only incapable of relishing or bearing part in any rational conversation, but of conceiving any generous, noble, or tender sentiment, and consequently of forming any just judgement concerning the many even of the ordinary duties of private life. ... His dexterity at his own particular trade seems to be acquired at the expense of his intellectual, social, and martial virtues. But in every improved and civilised society this is the state into which the labouring poor, that is, the great body of the people, must necessarily fall, unless government takes some pains to prevent it.

(*Ibid.*: 781–2)

As is clear from this passage, Smith observed the alienating effects of the factory system a century before Marx. The difference between the two passages from *The Wealth of Nations* is striking. The first seems to describe the division of labour in optimistic terms, as a great benefactor of productivity, and therefore of mankind, whereas the second is extremely dark and pessimistic, describing how the very process that increases productivity also destroys the workers as human beings by corrupting their moral and intellectual character. In that sense, *The Wealth of Nations* could be read as a tragedy.

The welfare of the poor was Smith's greatest concern. As he put it: "No society can surely be flourishing and happy, of which the far greater part of the members are poor and miserable" (*ibid.*: 96). Smith also argued that wages should be as high as possible, partly because of the welfare of the workers and partly because it would lead to economic growth. He criticized the existing poor laws because they did not allow the poor to live where they wanted to, and consequently sell their labour to whomever they wanted; these laws were clearly not for the benefit of the poor. He also argued that the state should pay for the education of the poor, to counteract the effects of their working conditions and in order for them to be able to let their voice be heard more in public debates. If Smith was such a good friend to the poor, how could he possibly defend the working conditions he described in the pin factory? The short answer is that he believed that this would, in the long run, serve the poor the most. Marx clearly had a more drastic approach in mind. Where Smith settled for a modest realism, hoping for a gradual improvement in the conditions for workers, Marx wanted something far more radical, namely the realization of the ideal of the communist society. This society is characterized by people freely choosing to do whatever they want to whenever they want to. As Marx puts it in *The German Ideology*:

> In communistic society, in which no one has an exclusive sphere of activity but can develop himself in any branch of activity, society regulates the general production and in doing so makes it possible for me to do this today, and that tomorrow, to go hunting in the morning and fishing in the afternoon. To tend the cattle in the evening and after supper to criticise, just as I wish, without ever becoming a hunter, fisherman, herdsman or critic.   ([1845] 1994: 132)

So you will primarily be a human being not a particular kind of worker, but you will still work, and as a direct expression of your self your work will be immensely satisfying. Marx envisaged working conditions that would "return" man to himself. It is the idea of a world in which human potential is fully realized. What sort of work are you supposed to be doing? It is not insignificant that none of the work mentioned in the quotation takes place in factories. One can argue that Marx's conception of work was outdated because he based it on the craftsmen of the Middle Ages rather than on industrial workers. If one were to implement Marx's ideal of work, one would probably have to close down all factories, given that workers in factories manufacture not complete products but rather a large number of parts that are later assembled. Given the nature of work in factories and Marx's conception of alienation, non-alienated factory work seems to be virtually impossible.

The non-alienated worker would be free. For Marx, freedom consists in fulfilling a certain ideal that is defined not by us as individuals, but in terms of our alleged human essence. Achieving true freedom will be about taking part in a collective process in which the "species essence" is realized. This is the reason for Marx's contempt for the "bourgeois liberty" of the liberal tradition, and his readiness to sacrifice the individual freedom warranted by constitutions. When one sets out to liberate mankind as a whole, the sacrifice of such freedoms seems to be a small price to pay.

In the early manuscripts Marx still places the realm of freedom in work, and he criticizes Adam Smith for only seeing freedom in leisure, but later he seems to have changed his mind. In the third volume of *Capital* he places work firmly within the "realm of necessity" and leisure becomes the "realm of freedom" (Marx [1894] 1993: part VII, ch. 48). The general gist of his argument is that any work that depends on needs, that is, is done from necessity, is not free, and that all work in fact depends on need; hence, there is no such thing as work that belongs to the realm of freedom. Freedom must be sought elsewhere. Marx recognizes that with growth in productivity it takes less work to satisfy a given need, but he also sees that human needs grow as a part of the civilizing process. Much of the gain in productivity will therefore be eaten up by the increase in needs. The pragmatic solution Marx proposes is that humans will have to continue working, and therefore remain in the realm of necessity, but that one can steadily attempt to reduce the amount of work and make it more "humane". The less pragmatic part of the solution is, of course, the communist revolution. Marx had faith in the revolution, and was somewhat sceptical towards efforts to improve the conditions of workers under capitalism because that improvement could mask the need for fundamental change, that is, the elimination of capitalism itself. As the essence of capitalism allegedly consisted of the exploitation of workers, it would be far better to let capitalism run its course, getting as ugly as possible, because that would presumably lead to a revolution.

It is interesting that the later Marx places the realm of freedom completely within leisure, whereas the younger Marx placed it within authentic or non-alienated work. Hence, the later Marx ends up with the very position that the younger Marx criticized

Smith for, in which human life is made up of unproductive freedom (leisure) and productive slavery (work). One could argue that by the time he wrote the third volume of *Capital*, Marx had come to realize that alienation would be an unavoidable aspect of work even under communism: that even under communism the "realm of freedom" could not be found anywhere but in leisure, whereas work would necessarily remain in the "realm of necessity". He does not address this question directly, but seems to have given up the idea of non-alienated work altogether. If we look at the conditions for workers in communist countries, there is little reason to believe that it is any less "alienated" than work in capitalist countries.

One could be tempted to say that, contrary to what Marx believed, the average worker's transition from the "realm of necessity" to the "realm of freedom" is achieved not by communism, but by capitalism. Could it be that the ideal of non-alienated work has become, if not fully realized, then at least a possibility in the capitalist, consumerist, late-modern society? Would it not be correct to say that work today contains more intrinsic satisfaction for more people than ever? Is it not the sort of work that lets people express who they are, something they can identify with as persons? A case could be made for such a point of view, but we should not get too carried away.

We often read and hear that work is so much more fulfilling these days because we can develop our talents and we have more freedom. In brief, work today is supposed to be quite a lot like what Aristotle described as leisure. But is it? Some work is and some is not. People who have what are often referred to as "McJobs" – typically flipping burgers in fast-food restaurants – can hardly be said to have vastly greater opportunities for developing their talents and finding meaning at work than typical workers in the old, industrial economy. The amount of intrinsic satisfaction is clearly not equally distributed among jobs. What about people working in offices, handling information all day long? The television series *The*

Office is a perfect illustration of how mind-numbingly boring and unfulfilling such work can be. Working at a call centre, taking call after call, or doing telemarketing, are contemporary versions of the assembly lines in Henry Ford's factories.

In the most optimistic portrayals of contemporary work, it seems as if every single worker is a member of what the American urban studies theorist Richard Florida has called the "creative class", which consists of people who engage in work whose function is to create "meaningful new forms" (Florida 2002: 5). That is hardly a clearly defined class, but Florida estimates that they make up approximately 30 per cent of the American workforce today. He further argues that the members of the creative class are bound together by "a common ethos that values creativity, individuality, difference and merit" (*ibid.*: 8). Having such an "ethos" is hardly an exclusive trait these days; I would say, rather, that it is as mainstream as you could possible get. Even though I am more than a little sceptical towards Florida's theory of the "creative class", it is still of some significance. One can say that the characteristics of this alleged class are precisely the same as those we described at the end of the previous chapter, with the Romantic transformation of the idea of work as a vocation. Rather than identifying a specific class, I would say that Florida has identified a widespread mentality or norm for what work *should* be like today. People in the "creative class" are the "model workers" of today; they are the ones who embody the Romantic ideal of self-realization 24/7, and such self-realization is supposed to be the very essence of meaning in life.

The obvious question now is: do these people in fact achieve self-realization and meaningful work? How well does this ideal correspond to the reality of work in late modernity? Flexibility has been a buzzword for some time. The new flexibility at work appears to give people more control over their lives because they are given more freedom to decide when and how to perform given tasks. But social scientist Richard Sennett argues the opposite and claims that control has been taken away from workers because flexibility has made their work life more unpredictable; as the workplace and working hours are destabilized, then so is the identity work can provide them with. Sennett argues that: "The conditions of time in the new capitalism have created a conflict between character and experience, the experience of disjointed time threatening the ability of people to form their characters into sustained narratives" (Sennett 1998: 31). There is some plausibility to Sennett's claim. My father belonged to a generation of workers who usually worked in one or two, at most three, organizations throughout their entire career. Even if they had to develop their skills as new technologies were introduced in the workplace – the most difficult for my father was probably learning to use a computer towards the end of his career – the general skill base was to a large extent the same throughout their careers. Today we are becoming nomads at work: constantly on the move, migrating from one job to another. While we are on the move, we are expected to pick up new skills and leave old ones behind. The idea of learning a basic set of skills that we continue to refine over a whole career seems outdated in the new economy. People who enter the workforce today, especially those with higher education, can expect to replace their entire skill base several times before they retire. On average, they will only spend a few years working in an organization before they move on to another, having to pick up new skills in their new jobs. Of course, learning new things can be exciting, but if we are constantly moving from one area to another we never get the opportunity to be really good at anything. There will be little depth to our skills.

One can argue that the difference between "permanent" and "temporary" jobs is becoming increasingly blurred. There are, of course, important differences between the two in terms of job security, but when we look at what people actually do and for how long they do it, "permanent" jobs are becoming more and more "temporary" and vice versa. Temporary work agencies existed in the 1860s, but it became a major industry only after the Second World War, and the largest growth has been in the past two decades. The most rapidly increasing group of workers in the Western world is people employed by temporary work agencies, and the largest private employer in the USA is one such agency, Manpower Inc. People in temporary jobs often show high job satisfaction at first, but as time goes by, as they become "permanent temps", this level of satisfaction has a tendency to drop. A friend of mine worked on short-term contracts for one of Norway's largest newspapers for more than four years. She was very happy at first because being a journalist for a large newspaper was her dream. As months became years and she still did not have a permanent job, never knowing if she would get another contract, having difficulties planning holidays, experiencing gaps between the contracts depending on the budgets in the newspaper and so on started to wear on her. One day she decided that she had had enough and refused to sign another short-term contract, which meant that she had to leave the newspaper. Her description was telling: "As I left the newspaper, I had a feeling of having left a boyfriend who had abused me for years. Fortunately, I have never had such a boyfriend, but I have been told that when you leave him, you cannot understand why you did not leave a long time ago." As a temp you do not manage to develop the same kind of "ownership" to your job as you have when you are permanently employed. It will be a less reliable source of meaning. What is more, as a temp you will usually do different things at each new job, so you have little opportunity to really learn to master anything. Temporary work and craftsmanship do not go very well together.

As we saw earlier, Marx modelled his idea of non-alienated – or meaningful – work on craftsmanship. One of the main reasons why the division of labour would make work less meaningful was that it undermined the very possibility of craftsmanship. How much skill can one develop in the art of drawing out wire, straightening it or cutting it, to use Smith's examples from the pin-factory? One can get better at it, and probably able to do it more and more efficiently, but that is a far cry from mastering a genuine craft. How much room for creativity is there? Very little, if any. How much of an expression of oneself can such handling of the wire amount to? The answer seems to be the same.

My first experience of being introduced to a craft was when I began working as a cleaning assistant. Some might argue that cleaning is not much of craft, which is something we associate more with such activities as carpentry, but, believe me, it is a craft! I worked as a cleaning assistant for eight years, and for five of those years I worked at Idun, a factory that produced ketchup, mustard, mayonnaise, salad dressing and so on. We started cleaning as soon as the production at the factory had shut down for the day, and we never knew how long our evenings would be. Sometimes we finished in a couple of hours and had most of the evening off, and other times we had to work past midnight. The work was hard, but the money was good and the guys I worked with were a lot of fun.

Most people would probably describe our work there as "low skilled", but I disagree. When I first began working there, my tasks were cleaning the floors and hosing down large metal containers. Then I moved on to cleaning the machinery, at first the smaller and simpler machines and later the larger and more complicated ones. We had to disassemble the machines, wash all the parts, grease them up and reassemble the parts again. The number of parts involved in the larger machines was quite intimidating; it was at least two years before I knew how to disassemble and reassemble all the machines in the factory. There was also a great variety of detergents, from the fairly normal soap to the ones that etched their way straight through one's skin if one did not use the correct protective gear. In addition there was the question of water temperature: for instance, one should not use very hot water to remove egg from a surface because it binds the protein and make it stick even harder. Some detergents could be mixed and others could not – should not –

because the cans could explode, which would be dangerous because some of these chemicals were pretty toxic. Working there was a crash course in applied chemistry. As new people were brought in, they would go through the same learning process as I had, starting with the simpler tasks and being rather closely supervised, being told and shown the right way to do something. As time went on, they would be given more and more autonomy as they started to show a proper understanding of the various tasks.

Looking back on the work we did, I would certainly not describe it as "low skilled"; it took years on the job to master it properly. I have had several so-called "high-skilled" jobs since then that have been far easier to master quickly. I would also describe the working environment as competitive. There was great pride involved in working quickly and yet producing flawless results. When our foreman looked over the work we had done at the end of the day, there was always a sense of shame if one of us had overlooked something or in some way done something that was not up to our standards. There was a general idea of craftsmanship, of getting it *right*.

After having cleaned for a couple of years, I was offered a job as a freelance sports reporter for a local newspaper. I accepted, which was a bad idea, since I turned out to be a terrible sports reporter: I had virtually no interest in sports, except for tennis and martial arts. My pieces on football were clearly lacking in enthusiasm for the sport. Since I was a bad sports reporter and a good cleaner, I chose to leave the newspaper and go back to cleaning. It was simply that I felt a greater sense of doing something worthwhile – and doing it well – when cleaning; doing a job well brings its own satisfaction.

Whenever we learn a craft, we are in a sense brought into a community that consists of all those who practise the relevant skills. We enter a social field governed by norms that we must obey. There is hardly any room for individual creativity in the beginning, as we must first master the basics. And we cannot learn the craft only by being *told* what to do; we have to learn it by *doing* it. This holds for carpentry and cleaning, as it does for doing science. Learning a craft has a lot to do with developing habits. To have a habit is to have a certain understanding of the world because it is a way of relating to the world.

The thing about learning a craft is that after a while we are able to do fairly complicated things with great ease, and that in itself is a source of great satisfaction. In this regard it differs little from, for instance, playing a sport such as tennis. One of the main reasons why playing tennis can be so enjoyable is that it is difficult, especially technically, and when we overcome those challenges and finally get the ball to behave the way we want it to, there is a truly profound pleasure to the activity. We even have days when everything "clicks": when we manage to do virtually everything with such ease that it seems as if we move about in a world without resistance. There is no distance between ourselves and the external world, but rather a fundamental unity. This sometimes happens when we are doing sport, but it can also happen at work. When we are fully immersed in work we lose our sense of having a distinct self and rather become one with the activity itself. Everything falls into place as we lose the sense of both time and self, and experience "flow". The world's leading theoretician on the experience of flow, the psychologist Mihály Csíkszentmihályi (1990), describes it as an optimal state for a person, where we are fully absorbed in what we are doing and find it completely motivating in itself, and not because it leads to something else. It is state of pure bliss. When we are "in the zone", we feel good. We become fully wrapped up in the activity itself. When work is at its best, we simply do not notice the passing of time at all; we are totally immersed in the present. When work is at its worst, time becomes a terrible burden. We watch the clock, hoping that it will speed up, but instead it seems to slow down more and more. We are also in the present in this situation, but it is bad kind of present. It is two completely different forms of the "now", two different experiences of time: in one time flies, and in the other it crawls.

One aspect of finding meaning in our work is enjoying the activity *in itself* while we are doing it. This kind of meaning usually fades pretty quickly. There is also the larger, more existential question as to the overall *point* of what we are doing, about whether we are in fact living a rich, meaningful life. This question certainly has a much wider range than work; it concerns our lives as a whole. Since work is such a crucial part of our lives, there is also the question of how our work fits in with our overall attempt to lead a meaningful life. We need some sort of purpose in our lives, and work is a part of that. As Bertrand Russell put it: "Consistent purpose is not enough to make life happy, but it is an almost indispensable condition of happy life. And consistent purpose embodies itself mainly in work" ([1930] 1996: 169). The question then is: what sort of consistent purpose are we ultimately looking for?

What about simply getting paid, for instance to support a family and provide your children with a good education? That is certainly a meaningful activity, a consistent purpose, but the meaning is here extrinsic to the work, in the form of wages, and not an intrinsic meaning. One might even say that there is no purpose to the job as such here, as it merely has instrumental value. The work makes no difference in itself; one could just as well have done any other job. If we are to experience our work as truly meaningful, there must also be something to be found in the job itself, some intrinsic meaning, not merely getting paid.

We want to make a difference to other people's lives. This also holds for our working lives. For most people it would probably be hard to stay in a job in which one did not in some sense believe that one made a positive contribution to the lives of others. The philosopher Hannah Arendt even argues that work can provide us mortals, living in a finite time that constantly floats away, with a measure of permanence and durability (Arendt 1958: 8ff.). In working, we leave a mark on the world: a mark that will hopefully outlive us, a testament to the fact that we have lived. If Arendt is correct, our perspective on work will ultimately extend beyond this life. We seem to have a need to leave a mark on the world, to show that we made some sort of difference.

This might seem like an exaggerated claim, as few of us have any illusion of leaving behind anything in our work that will be remembered for all eternity, or even for a considerably shorter time. However, I believe that Arendt's claim is not totally off the mark. In order to see why, let us take a quick look at Robert Nozick's famous argument about an experience machine in his book *Anarchy, State, and Utopia*:

> Suppose there were an experience machine that would give you any experience you desired. Superduper neuropsychologists could stimulate your brain so that you would think and feel you were writing a great novel, or making a friend, or reading an interesting book. All the time you would be floating in a tank, with electrodes attached to your brain. Should you plug into this machine for life, preprogramming your life's experiences? (Nozick 1974: 42)

It is an interesting question. In the context of work, you could have the most amazing – but fictional – career. You could earn your first doctorate at age 15 and your first Nobel Prize at 20. You could start your own company, which in two or three years becomes more valuable than Microsoft. Your inventions would be of enormous benefit to mankind, as they solve all problems of global warming and hunger. In brief, you could have a career that would easily make you the most important individual that has ever existed. If you should happen to prefer having a less eventful career in the experience machine, you could always choose to be a slacker instead. And you can fill in whatever details you like to make all other aspects of your life equally wonderful. The only drawback is, of course, that it would all be fictional. But you would not be aware of the unreality of your doings when you are plugged into the experience machine; it would all appear to be perfectly real to you, and you would be immensely satisfied with yourself. In fact, you could not possibly be more satisfied.

Would you let yourself be plugged into such a machine? Most people answer that they would not. A few, usually young students of philosophy, answer that they would. A well-known fictional example of someone who chooses to get plugged in is the character Cypher in the film *The Matrix*, who wishes to get reinserted into the matrix rather than to continue to live in what he sees as a miserable real world. Most people are appalled by the mere thought of such an existence, but why? I believe that the reason is simply that it would not be *real*. It would not amount to leaving a mark on the world. You must be able to see some *point* to what you are doing: the work must make some sort of *difference* in order to be meaningful. And nothing done in the experience machine would make a *real* difference. What is more, you would not contribute anything to the lives of others. Your existence would simply be of no real consequence.

Of course, we often fail to see the point of the things we spend a large part of our lives doing. Unlike the Protestants following Luther and Calvin, we also lack a grand metaphysics – or scheme of things – to fit our work into, which could serve as a guarantee that there *is* a point, even if we fail to fathom it ourselves. We suffer when our work fails to provide us with much meaning. At other times, our work seems to be immensely meaningful, so meaningful that virtually everything else in our lives fades in comparison, and we then tend to forget that work is only one source of meaning among others. The experience of work ranges over a continuum from deep personal fulfilment to utter boredom.

3. The distribution of work

Some jobs are more attractive than others and not all people find the same jobs equally attractive. Many people would probably have enjoyed being a sports reporter, with "perks" including free tickets, good seats and access to the athletes and managers. However, for someone like me with a meagre interest in sports, there was little reward in such a job, except for getting paid. It was not hard to fill the position after I left, so there were clearly others who wanted the job. There are probably more people who want to be sports reporters than there are available jobs. In the case of some jobs, the situation is the opposite: there are more jobs than there are people willing to do them. Some jobs are more sought after than others.

The labour market is not fair, if by "fair" we mean an equal distribution at work of internal (fun, self-realization, etc.) and external (wages, fringe benefits, etc.) goods. Both are clearly unequally distributed. Some jobs are higher in external than in internal goods and vice versa, and some are high in both or low in both. Sometimes you have to make a decision about what sort of goods are most important to you. As a teenager, my ambition was to become a stockbroker and make loads of money, but then I discovered philosophy and had a radical change of course in life. I changed course from a career that would be high in external goods, but perhaps not so high in internal ones, to a career that was significantly lower in external goods (although I am not complaining) but probably higher in internal ones. Since then I have been offered a few jobs that would pay significantly more than what I make as a philosopher, but none of them have seemed sufficiently attractive to me because they have seemed to contain significantly fewer internal goods. Some of these jobs might have been just as enjoyable and personally rewarding as philosophy has been for me, but I don't think so. I have been in a position where I could make a choice. Not everyone is in that position. A number of people end up with jobs that are low in both internal and external goods while others have the fortune to be able to choose the sort of jobs that are high in both kinds of goods. How can one justify such a difference in outcome?

This problem was addressed by Plato and Aristotle. On the one hand, the Greek philosophers found work to be a rather unworthy activity: something humans should be spared if they were to develop their human potential in a proper way. On the other hand, they also recognized that somebody actually had to *do* the different jobs, that is, that some people had to do the manual labour and that others had to be merchants. How can these two opinions be reconciled? That is far from clear. What is more, some jobs are taken to be more degrading than others, so the question is why particular people should have to do the most degrading jobs. This is a crucial question of social justice.

In the *Republic* Plato describes what he takes to be the ideal city-state. It is not discussed in very great detail, but the essentials are presented. It is interesting that a division of labour is one of the fundamental features. Plato argues that people do a better job if they specialize than if they perform all sorts of tasks (*Republic*, 374a–c). The crucial question is how the various jobs are to be distributed among the citizens of the state. Since Plato is attempting to describe an *ideal* state, which is supposed to be completely just, the distribution must also be fully rational and fair. A person cannot be told to become a manual labourer simply because of the whims of the rulers or because of a completely arbitrary procedure, such as a lottery. The reason Plato gives for why a person should be given a certain job rather than another is that different people have different talents: "One man is naturally fitted for one task, and another for another" (370a–b). The jobs would be distributed such that those with weak bodies would become merchants and those with weak minds would become manual labourers; he does not tell us what those with weak bodies *and* weak minds are supposed to do. He claims that people are born with given talents. Plato thinks in terms of a fixed essence in each and every human being that makes them suitable for one kind of work rather than another, and he further believes that it is one's duty towards the city-state to do the job one is the most suited to by nature: "each one man must perform one social service in the state for which his nature was best adapted" (433a). We are all obliged to serve the common good, according to Plato. The problem, of course, is that the sort of life that Plato describes does not appear to be very desirable. Utopias generally come across as uninhabitable for real human beings, and Plato's ideal state is no exception.

Aristotle places less emphasis on the overall idea of the common good and more on the individual. That might at first lead us to believe that his account would be more attractive to the modern reader, but this is hardly the case. How can Aristotle reconcile the ideas that work must be done and that work is incompatible with living a fully virtuous and happy life? His solution is slavery (*Politics* Bk 1.3–7). The work done by slaves made a life of leisure available for the likes of Aristotle.

Aristotle argued that slavery could be justified; in fact, his ethics more or less presupposes slavery. A fundamental premise in Aristotle's ethics is that for a person to develop proper virtue he must have vast amounts of leisure time at his disposal, and that time is available only if somebody else does the work. The only alternative to slavery would be to have all work done by means of machinery. This was actually Oscar Wilde's later solution to the problem in *The Soul of Man under Socialism* (Wilde [1891] 2001: 140ff.), but a technological solution was clearly not on Aristotle's intellectual horizon. And had Aristotle been able to conceive of a society in which machines took care of all production, he would probably have been strongly opposed to it, given the general distrust of technology among the ancient Greeks. Aristotle therefore had no option other than to defend the institution of slavery, given his overall ethical and political thought. The question is, of course, how on earth such a vile institution could be defended.

Aristotle's defence is simple: some people are "natural slaves", and since the good life for each and every being consists in living in accordance with their nature, slavery will in fact be the good life for these people (*Politics* 1254). They are, he argues, better off as slaves than as free men. The very idea of "natural slaves" is preposterous to the modern reader, but even if one accepts this untenable premise, there is still a problem with Aristotle's argument: how could one possible distinguish between the "natural slaves" and free men? After all, people are not born with the word "slave" written across their foreheads. As Aristotle was also well aware, slaves were often captives from the losing side of a war, and it would be a strange coincidence if the people who lost a given war simply happened to be slaves by nature. Even Aristotle admitted this, and he wrote that those who are opposed to slavery because it is unjust are to some extent correct (1255). We would expect him, then, to take the consequence of this insight and protest against this unjust institution, but he didn't. On the contrary, he took slavery to be a necessary injustice. He seemed to think: somebody has to do the dirty work, and it had better not be me.

Even though Plato's and Aristotle's theories are unacceptable for us today, the problems they address are still with us: the difficulty of finding the "right job" for a person – the job that suits their "nature"; and the fact that some people will be stuck with the least attractive jobs. The same problems were addressed in Aldous Huxley's dystopic novel, *Brave New World* (1932), in which various worker types are genetically engineered to fit certain roles. One could argue, for instance, that the Epsilons, who work on production lines and have no conception of any other sort of life, are the artificially produced equivalent to Aristotle's "natural slaves", whereas the Alphas would correspond to the aristocrats.

An individual's wishes for his or her work life are not necessarily compatible with the needs of society. When children are asked about what they want to become when they grow up, very few reply that they dream of working in the sewers or stacking supermarket shelves. To some extent childhood preferences remain with them as they grow up, even though they start to consider a greater range of desirable and undesirable jobs. Some of them will ultimately end up doing jobs they have little desire for. Who will take the least attractive jobs? Somebody has to. I am not arguing that working in the sewers or stacking supermarket shelves are in any way "unrespectable" jobs. I am merely saying that such jobs will typically be had by people who have a smaller range of choices than others, and that they are to some extent "stuck" with jobs with fewer internal and external goods.

On what basis should people be given one job rather than another? The most obvious answer would seem to be: on the basis of their qualifications. This is a *meritocratic* idea. The only other options would seem to be some form of nepotism, quotas or a completely random procedure, such as a lottery. The advantages of meritocracy over the other options are, first, that it seems *fair* to give someone a job because they contribute more. Secondly, it is clearly more *efficient* to give the job to the most qualified person because he or she will contribute the most. It is not obvious that the argument about fairness holds water. People can contribute more because they are more talented or because they work harder. Working harder than somebody else clearly has merit, but is that also the case with having a certain talent? Why should someone be rewarded simply because nature has endowed them with a talent? After all, having that talent is not a result of personal achievement. If John is twice as talented as Paul, but only works at 60 per cent of his capacity, whereas Paul pushes himself to the limit, John will still be slightly more productive than Paul. Would we not be inclined to think of Paul as more deserving than John, even though John contributes more? We would usually think that an ordinary person who gives £100 to charity is more praiseworthy than a billionaire who does the same. So the argument from fairness might not be totally convincing. However, in practice it will be extremely difficult to establish the ratio between hard work and talent that goes into producing an end result, so we will probably have to just look at the end result. And the argument from efficiency will still hold. So it seems that a meritocratic order is preferable to its alternatives.

A basic idea in liberal democracies is that there should be a basic equality of opportunity. If we had a society with fully equal opportunities, one would expect to find a lot of social mobility from one generation to the next. This is not the case. If you look at various labour market statistics you find patterns: children reproduce their parent's working careers: blue-collar parents have blue-collar children who take blue-collar jobs; women continue to take typical "women's jobs"; immigrants continue to do the kinds of low-paid service jobs that immigrants have traditionally done. Of course, there are many exceptions; many immigrants are climbing the corporate ladder, and half of all the management and professional jobs in the United States today are held by women. But the general picture is still that the social differentiations in the field of work really have not changed as much as we used to believe. Several studies from various countries even indicate that social mobility is actually dropping, and that young people who enter the workforce today are less likely to move up in the social hierarchy than their parents were. There is no strict determinism at play here – one's social position at birth is not one's destiny – but we are shaped by our social environment to a greater extent than we tend to recognize.

Not only the choice of profession, but also whether or not one in fact has a job runs in the family. The mere existence of unemployment appears to violate Article 23 of the Universal Declaration of Human Rights, which states that everyone has a *right* to work. The article leaves ample room for interpretation, but I will not go into technicalities here. Is a general right to work a good idea? No Western nation has ever granted such a positive right to work for all citizens. There is good reason why: it makes little sense from an economic point of view because it would hardly be very efficient. Someone might say that full employment is more important than efficiency, in which case they would be thinking along the same lines as Chairman Mao. There is a story of a Western economist in China under Mao. He visits a site where hundreds of workers are building a huge dam using shovels. He asks why they do not use an excavator. The foreman replies that using such mechanical tools would mean that the people using shovels would lose their jobs. The economist then says: "I thought that you were building a dam. If you want to create jobs, you should take away their shovels and give them spoons." It is true that using spoons instead of shovels or excavators would create jobs. The problem is that these jobs would not be very productive. That would in turn mean that these jobs would contribute very little to the general prosperity of the nation, and they would not contribute to raising the general standard of living, something the workers themselves in turn would have to suffer.

Even if everybody were to be granted the right to work, they would not necessarily get a job they would like. One could imagine that the state would employ an army of street cleaners. Of course, the streets would be clean, but it is unlikely that all those who clean the streets would be very happy with the job. A right to work cannot be a right to one's preferred job. I cannot have the right to be a Formula 1 driver, or to be a megalomaniac artist who is guaranteed funds to produce monumental art projects that will dwarf Christo and Jeanne-Claude's wrapping of the German Reichstag. Many people wanted to direct the film trilogy *The Lord of the Rings*, films with a budget of several hundred million dollars, but only Peter Jackson got to do it. Very few of those who dream of becoming jetfighter pilots end up flying jetfighters. Of course, plans also change. Many of those who dreamt of becoming pilots when they were young found other interests and went in other directions. Some got jobs in which they could realize their personal ambitions and others did not. A universal right to work is probably a bad idea, and it might not be something to yearn for either, since it would not be a right to a job one would like to have.

This might not seem fair, but it is hard to see how it could be otherwise. In an ideal world, it would perhaps be possible to have a completely equal distribution of work-related goods, but we do not live in an ideal world. As William James pointed out:

> If the ethical philosopher were only asking after the best *imaginable* system of goods he would indeed have an easy task; for all demands as such are *prima facie* respectable, and the best simply imaginary world would be one in which *every* demand was gratified as soon as made. Such a world would, however, have to have a physical constitution entirely different from that of the one which we inhabit. (1915: 201)

Even attempting to bring our societies close to such an ideal of an equal distribution of both kinds of goods might not be a good idea. Societies that have attempted to realize a completely equal distribution, especially of the external goods, have usually ended up being societies in which all parties – except for the members of "the Party" – have less of all sorts of goods. It might be a more equal society, but hardly a better one. This is not to say that vast inequalities are in any sense desirable, and there is definitely room for concern about rising inequalities in recent years, but a society in which one attempts to eliminate all inequalities is probably a far worse alternative.

4. Work and leisure

It has become increasingly common to argue that we work too much these days, and that the amount of work we have to put in makes us burned out or even sends us to an early grave. Neil Young may be right when he sings: "It's better to burn out, than to fade away" (Young 1979). I guess that most of us would prefer not to do either, and rather live a full life without burning the candle at both ends. Does work send us to an early grave? Do we even work all that much? Contrary to popular claims, we actually work less than ever before, and the work we do is even beneficial for our physical and mental health.

Compared to working hours 200 years ago, or even just 50 years ago, most of us work "part-time" today. People working in top- and middle-management – executives, lawyers, and so on – put in significantly more hours at work than the average worker, but generally also many fewer hours than the typical worker a century or two ago. Let us start with a really grim picture. The British Factory Act of 1833 aimed to reduce the working hours for adults and children in the textile industry. For those older than thirteen it stipulated a twelve-hour working day between the hours of 5.30am and 8.30 pm, whereas children aged nine to thirteen were to work a nine-hour day. Of course, this sounds insane today, but factory owners even broke that law, forcing both adults and children to work longer hours. Only workaholics would regularly put in such hours today, and we certainly do not accept child labour. Since the Industrial Revolution, the average Western worker has spent fewer hours at work. We have to go back to pre-modern times to find a society where the average worker worked less.

Descriptions of the huge amount of work we allegedly do today are often contrasted with a rosy picture of the harmonious lives of hunter-gatherers who devote significantly fewer hours to work: the Kapauku of Papua never work two days in a row, the !Kung of the Kalahari Desert never work more than fifteen hours per week and Australian Aborigines traditionally worked at most four hours per day. In *Stone Age Economics*, the anthropologist Marshall Sahlins describes hunter-gatherers as "the original affluent society" ([1972] 2003). Their affluence is not one of material wealth, however, but of time. If you are tempted by such a lifestyle, you should realize that these groups are extremely poor by our material standards. Each and every one of us could work much less if we simply settled for a lower standard of living. Of course, we would not be in the same situation as the hunter-gatherers if we worked only half the hours we do now; we would still be far better off. Since general productivity has doubled in the past fifty years, we should – in principle – be able to work half the hours and have exactly the same standard of living as people had just fifty years ago. Almost certainly we would not be happy with that standard of living so we have to put in more hours at work.

If we move on from hunter-gatherers to the classical world, we find that people living then had a lot of leisure time. In ancient Greece festivals were so numerous that one wonders if time was ever found between them for work. Of course, slaves worked during the festivals, which explains how society could actually function in spite of all the leisure time. The situation was essentially the same for the Romans, who had as much as 175 days every year reserved for festivals. The Roman festivals were transformed to Christian holy days in the Middle Ages, so there was plenty of time off work then too.

We should not romanticize life in earlier times, despite the leisure time, because it was full of hardship. A significant explanation for the short working hours in earlier societies is that most people did not have the stamina to work longer; their calorie intake was so meagre that it could only support so many hours of work and this work was done at a much slower pace. In the long run, you cannot get more energy out of a human body than what you put into it. Our current calorie intake, on the other hand, is so high that most of us do not burn it up at work, and consequently either have to exercise after work to get rid of the surplus energy or become seriously overweight.

The really long working week is a much more recent phenomenon, linked to modern capitalism. The story of capitalism up until the second half of the nineteenth century is one of constantly increasing working hours. From being lower than today's working hours in the Middle Ages it rose to nearly twice as much as our current levels, peaking around 1850. There was also a decline in the number of holidays. One important reason for why the number of hours continued to rise for so long was that workers were paid by the day, and not by the hours. The number of hours rose faster than the daily wages because the factory owners made more of a profit that way, and the workers were not able to put up much of a protest. Eventually a new system of payment by the hour was introduced, and longer hours then gave higher wages. This also meant that it was not necessarily in the interest of the factory-owners to squeeze as many hours as possible out of the workers, as the last few hours – when the workers were tired – would not be as profitable as the earlier hours.

Between 1850 and today, average working hours in advanced OECD countries have been reduced by almost 50 per cent. For a while, it seemed as if we were working our way steadily towards the ideal presented in Paul Lafargue's *The Right To Be Lazy*, which recommended that we should not have to work more than three hours per day. However, the steady decline in working hours seems to have slowed down, and in some countries – including the USA and the UK – there even seems to have been a slight increase.

Determining exactly how much we work today is far from easy, and the numbers vary considerable according to the source. The numbers from the OECD on average working hours per year are the most widely quoted, and at present they are: 1777 in the USA; 1717 in Canada; 1652 in the UK; 1541 in Ireland; 1362 in Germany; and 1346 in France. We see that the differences between countries are significant, with Americans working 431 and Brits 306 hours more than the French. On the other hand, the difference between Americans and Brits is only 125 hours. This might come as a surprise, since European media have a tendency to present a nightmarish picture of work life in the USA. For instance, one can often get the impression that a great number of Americans must have two or three jobs just to get by. If one investigates the actual numbers, a far less dramatic picture emerges. In 2003, 5.3 per cent of Americans in the workforce had more than one job, and only 0.2 per cent had two full-time jobs (Gersemann 2005: 123). In fact, the number of workers with more than one job has been going down in the past decade. There is also a clear correlation between the level of education and the number of jobs: people with higher education are far more likely to have more than one job.

How much does the average American actually work? That is a difficult question to answer because estimates vary considerably, from lower than forty hours per week to higher than fifty. The truth is probably somewhere in the middle, but the actual number of hours is a highly disputed issue. It depends on how you choose to measure it and how much you include in the concept of work. If you use a very wide concept of work, you will also get a high number of hours. This is certainly the case with Juliet Schor's *The Overworked American* (1991). Schor includes all sorts of non-paid activities in her definition of work, such as cooking, cleaning your house, taking care of houseplants, gardening, childcare, helping your children with their homework, reading to or conversing with your children, taking care of your pets, washing your car, shopping for groceries and other

household items and so on. Given such an extremely wide definition of work, virtually nothing is excluded from that category. I
guess that watching television will not be work according to such
a definition, unless you watch it with your children. And going to
a cafe with a friend or having a game of tennis will not be considered work. Virtually everything you do not do exclusively for your
own benefit – and even some of the things you do only for yourself,
such as making a meal only for your own consumption – seems to
be regarded as work. No wonder Schor's estimates of the average
American's working hours are remarkably high. What is more, since
Schor clearly believes that too much of this thing she refers to as
"work" is bad for you, one wonders what her ideas of the good life
would be like. Is it one where you do not have to read to your children
or take care of your pets, and can give your full attention to yourself?
If so, her idea of the good life differs significantly from mine.

A problem with many studies of working hours is that they are
based on people's own estimates, and we tend to overestimate the
number of hours we work. In a study of how Americans spend their
time, John Robinson and Geoffrey Godbey asked 10,000 survey
participants to keep a diary of their days, minute by minute, twenty-
four hours a day. The results reported in the book *Time for Life*
(1997) were remarkable. The men in the survey claimed that they
worked on average 46.2 hours per week, but when the researchers
added up their diary entries, it turned out that they in fact only
worked 40.4 hours per week. The discrepancy was even larger in the
case of women, who claimed to work 40.4 hours per week, when
their diary entries only showed 32 hours. The more people claimed
to work, the larger were the discrepancies. People, who claimed
that they worked as much as 80 hours per week, did in fact work
55 hours according to their time diaries. That is still quite a lot, but
significantly less than they claimed. In fact, the study concluded that
Americans have more time for leisure than ever before. Even if one
included commuting and unpaid tasks at home, such as cleaning

and cooking, total work time amounted to no more 50 hours per week, and that leaves more time for leisure than Americans have ever had before.

Even though the average working hours are generally not increasing – and in those few countries where there might be an increase, it is fairly small – the number of people who claim to work significantly more than average hours is on the rise. So even though most people work less than before, a minority seems to work increasingly more and the size of this minority seems to increase. In fact, one in six workers in the UK claims to work more than 60 hours a week. These people might expose themselves to a health risk due to over-work. A few studies indicate that people working very long hours – upwards of twelve hours a day – have a significantly increased risk of injury and illness. That should not come as a surprise to anyone. Some people actually work themselves to death.

There is no single word in English for working oneself to death. The Japanese word is *karoshi* and the Chinese word is *guolasi*. In Japan this is recognized as a serious problem, and the ministry of labour publishes annual statistics on death from *karoshi*. There is even a trend of *karoshi* lawsuits, in which the deceased's family demands compensation from the employer. There are also examples of death from overwork in Europe and the US, but there are no official numbers. One cannot argue from this that a reduction in today's average working hours in the Western countries will have any health benefit. Of course, work will not kill you if you don't work, but something else will. As John Maynard Keynes pointed out: "In the long run, we are all dead" ([1923] 2000: 80).

People in the workforce generally live longer than people outside it. In Norway the difference is as high as eight years for women and seven for men. This difference can be explained in different ways – for instance, by the fact that a large number of people are outside the workforce because they suffer from various illnesses – but there is no support for the claim that work generally leads on to an earlier encounter with the grim reaper. In fact, the opposite seems to be the case.

Naturally, this will in individual cases depend on exactly what sort of work one does, but in general there is solid evidence for the health benefits of work. The most comprehensive survey of this matter to date, *Is Work Good for Your Health and Well-Being?* by British medical professors Gordon Waddell and A. Kim Burton, concludes that "work is generally good for physical and mental health and well-being" (2006: ix). Their study is interesting because they take the opposite approach to the common one in which one investigates the adverse effects of work on health and therefore has assumed at the outset that work is to be conceived of as a health hazard. By focusing on the beneficial aspects of work, a completely different picture emerges.

Unemployment is a far bigger health hazard than work. In developed countries with a fair level of social security, the psychological aspects of unemployment seem to be the most important, and they have a serious impact on people's health in terms of higher mortality and poorer physical and mental health. In terms of a negative effect on happiness, or "subjective well-being" as it is often called in empirical studies, unemployment is one of the things with the highest impact, along with serious illness and divorce. It seems that loss of income is only a minor part of this, and that other factors have greater impact than the purely economic ones. The "typical" unemployed will have less social interaction with others and lower self-esteem. People take unemployment personally. They experience it as something that affects them as individuals, not only as members of the group "the unemployed". Given how much emphasis we place on work as a source of identity, it should come as no surprise that people are often devastated when they lose their jobs and fail to find a new one.

The most surprising result in Waddell and Burton's study is perhaps that those who suffer from declining physical and mental health while being unemployed regain their health when they find work. They argue that there might be a group of approximately 5–10 per cent of the population who might have better health if they stay out of work, especially those with asthma and severe illness, but the rest of us will generally get a health benefit from working. The fact that work in general has a beneficial effect on health and longevity does not imply that one will have even better health and live even longer if one works more. Too much work is destructive. It is no coincidence that labour camps are institutions for punishment. It is hard to determine how much "too much work" is, but from a health perspective there is no reason to think that people today generally work "too much".

Another indication that most people do not – after everything – believe that they work too much is that so few are willing to work part-time. Many companies offer their employees part-time work, with a corresponding pay cut, but study after study show that that very few employees, usually 3–5 per cent, take the offer. The question is why. For some employees the answer is simply that they cannot afford a pay cut if they want to maintain a decent standard of living. However, the employees with a high income, who could cut down on their working hours and wages and still be well above the median income, are no more willing to cut down. In fact, they are even less likely than those with lower income even to take the *paid* holidays they are entitled to. Again, the question is why. Some might fear that they will be more exposed to redundancy if they do not show their full commitment to the company by putting in full hours and more, but the number of workers who choose to work shorter hours does not increase when the economy is going well and the risk of being laid off is in fact very low. Another worry is that we will have less chance of being promoted if we only work part-time. That seems more likely. If I were to promote someone and had the choice between two equally qualified employees, where one works full-time and the other part-time, I would probably go for the full-time employee. I guess that the question one must ask oneself is how important the possibility of such a promotion really is. If we think that spending more time with our family and friends is of great importance to us, missing out on a promotion should be an acceptable price to pay. Some might say that it is unfair that people get "punished" for wanting to spend more time with their families. In my view they do not get punished, but simply make a choice about what truly matters to them; I believe that they get the better deal in the long run than the people who miss out on so much of their family life.

The most plausible explanation for why people do not work shorter hours, even when they can, is simply that they do not in fact want shorter hours. In her interesting study of the current relations between work and family life, *The Time Bind*, Arlie Russell Hochschild cites two studies which both indicate this (Hochschild 2000: 33ff.). In 1985 the US Bureau of Labor Statistics conducted a survey where they asked workers whether they would prefer a shorter working week, a longer one or if they wanted to keep their present one. Less than 10 per cent replied that they wanted shorter hours; 65 per cent said that they wanted to keep their present hours and the rest actually wanted *longer* hours. A 1993 study by the Families and Work Institute in New York asked a large number of workers how much time and energy they devoted to work, family and friends and themselves, and followed up with a question about how much time they ideally would like to spend on each of these. The replies to the two questions were nearly identical. If these studies give a fairly correct picture of what people generally think about the work–life balance, it seems that people believe that they have found this balance, or at least that they are close.

The seemingly widespread opinion that workers in the Western world are generally working themselves to death, or at least are in constant danger of breaking down from overwork, finds very little support in the available studies. It appears to be nothing but a popular myth. One might argue that even though we work fewer hours than in the recent past, the intensity and pace has increased, but there is little evidence for this. The overall intensity of our lives seems to have increased, however. We sleep less than we used to. Over the past century the average amount of sleep has declined by 1–2 hours a day, which is quite significant. What do we do with our extra time awake? One thing is certain: we do not spend it at work. And yet more and more people complain about being worn out, or even burnt out. If that is the case, the most plausible explanation seems to be that we are not worn out by work, but rather by leisure.

The proverb "All work and no play, makes Jack a dull boy" – today perhaps best known through Stanley Kubrick's film *The Shining* – can be traced back as far as to James Howell's *Proverbs* (1659). The general idea is far older, and in the maxims of the Egyptian sage Ptah-Hotep, written in the twenty-fourth century BCE, one can read: "One that reckons accounts all the day passes not a happy moment". The "Father of History", Herodotus, writes that the Egyptian pharaoh Amasis replied in the following way when some of his friends accused him of being too much of a slacker:

> Bowmen bend their bows when they wish to shoot; unbrace them when the shooting is over. Were they kept always strung they would break, and fail the archer in time of need. So it is with men. If they give themselves constantly to serious work, and never indulge awhile in pastime or sport, they lose their senses, and become mad or moody. Knowing this, I divide my life between pastime and business.   (Herodotus 1996: 191)

That is perfectly sound advice 2500 years later as well. Everybody needs to relax every now and then. Ford was of the opposite opinion: "None of us has any right to ease. There is no place in civilization for the idler" (Ford & Crowther [1922] 2003: 13). He was wrong, of course. The necessity of rest is even maintained in Article 24 of the Universal Declaration of Human Rights, which states: "Everyone has the right to rest and leisure, including reasonable limitation of working hours and periodic holidays with pay".

The word "leisure" stems from the Latin *licere*, which means to be permitted. In our leisure time we are permitted to spend our hours as we please. At least that seems to be the basic idea of what leisure is about. Whether or not a particular activity is work or leisure will then depend on the attitude of the person doing it: professional athletes are clearly working when they are performing their sport, but many of us do sports in our leisure time; reading books is something I usually regard as work, but counts as leisure for most people; if I were to make a bookcase it would probably be leisure, but it would be work for a carpenter. We might say that one man's work is another man's leisure.

This point is made clear in Mark Twain's *Adventures of Tom Sawyer*, in the famous scene where Tom manages to trick all his friends into whitewashing a fence for him by making them believe that whitewashing in fact is a rare opportunity. He even gets them to pay him for the privilege with tin-soldiers and firecrackers:

> He had discovered a great law of human action, without knowing it – namely, that in order to make a man or a boy covet a thing, it is only necessary to make the thing difficult to attain. If he had been a great and wise philosopher, like the writer of this book, he would now have comprehended that Work consists of whatever a body is obliged to do, and that Play consists of whatever a body is not obliged to do. And this would help him to understand why constructing artificial flowers or performing on a tread-mill is work, while rolling ten-pins or climbing Mont Blanc is only amusement. There are wealthy gentlemen in England who drive four-horse passenger-coaches twenty or thirty miles on a daily line, in

the summer, because the privilege costs them considerable money; but if they were offered wages for the service, that would turn it into work and then they would resign.

([1876] 2006: 23–4)

If your attitude can make work into leisure, the opposite would also seem to be possible: your attitude can turn leisure into work. What should leisure be like? Most people would agree that it should be playful. The word "play" stems from the Latin *plega*, which means to dance or rejoice. Playful activities are *autotelic*, which means that they have no end beyond themselves. Of course, playful activities can have many beneficial effects, but that is not our *reason* for engaging in them. We play because it is fun.

And yet it is clear that much of what passes for leisure is not much fun at all. In *Beyond Good and Evil*, Friedrich Nietzsche writes:

> The industrious races find it extremely difficult to tolerate idleness; it was a stroke of genius on the part of the *English* instinct to spend Sundays in tedium with a *te deum* so that English people would unconsciously lust for their week- and workdays. ([1886] 2001: §189)

Today we seem to have gone to the opposite extreme, filling up all our leisure time with so many activities that it is virtually bursting. Leisure has become so demanding these days that getting back to work often appears to be the true vacation. There is much empirical evidence to suggest that more and more people actually prefer spending more time at work because they find their time off work so stressful. Companies are going to great lengths to provide their employees – especially in management – with services that make it possible for them to spend more hours at work and fewer at home. Many people do not see their homes as a place where they are free from work, but rather as their second workplace, and a less rewarding one. According to Hochschild (1997), this holds more for women than for men. The overall differences are not very big, but men are in "a positive emotional state" at home more often than women, whereas the opposite holds for the emotional state at work. It is hardly a daring hypothesis to think that this is related to the distribution of chores at home.

Several writers claim that they prefer work over leisure. In *The Conquest of Happiness* Bertrand Russell argues:

> Work therefore is desirable, first and foremost, as a prevention of boredom, for the boredom that a man feels when he is doing necessary though uninteresting work is nothing in comparison with the boredom that he feels when he has nothing to do with his days. ([1930] 1996: 163)

He goes on to argue that "even the dullest work is to most people less painful than idleness" (*ibid.*). This claim is somewhat surprising, as one of Russell's most famous essays is entitled "In Praise of Idleness", and he appears to directly contradict the argument in that essay. I believe that he is right, however, in arguing that work is often less painful than utter idleness.

In *De Homine*, Thomas Hobbes writes: "Work is good; it is truly a motive for life. Therefore unless you walk for the sake of walking, you do so for your work. *Where shall I turn, what shall I do?* are the voices of people grieving. Idleness is torture" ([1657] 1991: 51). On a similar note, Noël Coward claimed that "Work is much more fun than fun". Is it true? It depends on what sort of work and what sort of fun one is having. If you conducted a survey among all the workers of the world, I doubt that the majority of them would agree with Coward. On the other hand, a large number of them would probably also agree that fun would not be as much fun without work. If you have the entire week off, the weekend is not anything special. In 1996 the Copenhagen Institute for Future Studies asked a large number of Danes about whether work or leisure was the most fulfilling, or if they were equally fulfilling (cf. Jensen 2001). Ten per cent of the respondents answered that work was the most fulfilling, 13 per cent that it was leisure and the overwhelming majority of 77 per cent replied that they were equally fulfilling. The majority was probably on to something there. Having only one without the other makes it less valuable, whereas having both increases the value of both.

In an article of 1928, G. K. Chesterton pointed out that "leisure" can have different meanings:

I think the name of leisure has come to cover three totally different things. The first is being allowed to do something. The second is being allowed to do anything. And the third (and perhaps most rare and precious) is being allowed to do nothing. Of the first we have undoubtedly a vast and a very probably a most profitable increase in recent social arrangements. Undoubtedly there is much more elaborate equipment and opportunity for golfers to play golf, for bridge-players to play bridge, for jazzers to jazz, or for motorists to motor. But those who find themselves in the world where these recreations are provided will find that the modern world is not really a universal provider. He will find it made more and more easy to get some things and impossible to get others. The second sort of leisure is certainly not increased, and is on the whole lessened. The sense of having a certain material in hand which a man may mould into any form he chooses, this is a sort of pleasure now almost confined to artists. As for the third form of leisure, the most precious, the most consoling, the most pure and holy, the noble habit of doing nothing at all – that is being neglected in a degree which seems to me to threaten the degeneration of the whole race. It is because artists do not practice, patrons do not patronise, crowds do not assemble to

worship reverently the great work of Doing Nothing, that the
world has lost its philosophy and even failed to create a new
religion.   (1970: 271)

It is somewhat ironic that Chesterton himself wrote more than 100
books, and was therefore utterly incapable of "Doing Nothing". I
believe that we are even worse off today than Chesterton was when
he wrote this passage 70 years ago, and we should perhaps add a
fourth meaning: having to do everything!

The weekend and holidays especially are approached with a sense
of urgency. It is a limited time that should be utilized to the full, not
wasted. Strict time management does not seem to be compatible
with anything even resembling a holiday. It strikes me that our holidays increasingly resemble a sort of tyranny of efficiency. The bus-
loads of tourists that seem to stop for approximately fifteen minutes
at every new sight, thereby maximizing the number of sights seen,
are becoming the norm.

Another word for holiday, "vacation", stems from Latin *vacation* or *vacatio* which means freedom and exemption. A vacation is supposed to be about what you choose to do, as opposed
to what you are obliged to do. Yet vacations often turn into a kind
of job – the sort you have to pay for yourself – where not a single
minute should be wasted, where you "must" see this museum or
that monument. I personally prefer vacations that are a complete
waste of time, as that for me is the essence of being on holiday. Since
I travel quite a lot in the line of philosophical duty, giving lectures
in various countries, the best vacation for me is often simply being
able to stay at home, doing virtually nothing, not having to go to
another airport and check into another hotel.

The temporality of work has invaded our leisure, making it a lot
like work, and "real work" can often appear to be a relief compared
to the "pseudo-work" of our leisure. Leisure can take a toll on us,
as to an increasing degree we spend it as if Benjamin Franklin was

indeed correct in his claim that "time is money" (1987: 320). We are keeping tighter and tighter schedules in our leisure. One might say that we implicitly structure leisure time as if we were following nineteenth-century management consultant F. W. Taylor's principles of scientific management. Leisure time is to be used as efficiently as possible. We are outsourcing childcare, cleaning, cooking and so on in order to preserve as much of our precious leisure time as possible, only to become even more hectic. In terms of appointments, of doing this and that at a specified time, many people's leisure time is in fact more structured than their work time. If your leisure is ruled by a time planner, it is not really leisure, is it?

The nineteenth-century philosopher and sociologist Herbert Spencer warned Americans about this in a lecture he gave in New York in 1882:

> Exclusive devotion to work has the result that amusements cease to please; and, when relaxation becomes imperative, life becomes dreary from lack of its sole interest – the interest in business. The remark current in England that, when the American travels, his aim is to do the greatest amount of sight-seeing in the shortest time, I find current here also: it is recognized that the satisfaction of getting on devours nearly all other satisfactions.   (1891: 483)

In the same lecture, he states that: "It is time to preach the gospel of relaxation" (*ibid.*: 486). Our leisure has become decreasingly relaxing in the past 125 years. We all increasingly resemble the Americans he describes in his lecture. As far as I can see, the main reason why so many people today complain about being worn out, burnt out and so on, is not that their work is so hard, but rather that their leisure is.

5. Being managed

Except for the self-employed very few workers can avoid the phenomenon of management. The verb "to manage" stems from the Italian *maneggiare*, which means to handle, and it was especially used to describe the handling of horses. The noun "management" has retained some of the meaning that somebody is leading somebody or something else, although the actual handling at work these days tends to be more verbal than physical.

Exactly when management became a factor in work is a matter of dispute. Some see it as a distinctly modern phenomenon, whereas others stress that some form of management was already part of the organization of work among the ancient Sumerians and Egyptians. One can also argue that the military drilling in Spartan and Roman society – in order to maximize efficiency – bears some resemblance to "scientific management". However, it is clear that work planning became a much more important phenomenon when more and more work was done in factories.

The major breakthrough for the scientific study of management came with F. W. Taylor's *Principles of Scientific Management* (1911), which is probably one of the most influential books of the modern world. It may have had a limited number of readers, but it changed the entire outlook on how work in the modern world should be managed in order to maximize output. Taylor was a notoriously hard worker, getting up at 5am, working from 7am to 5pm, then walking home for dinner before studying until 11pm; he then went jogging before he went to bed and indulged himself with a full five hours of sleep. This was clearly a man who allowed neither himself nor others any slack.

Taylor employed a cutting-edge technology of his day: the stopwatch. His experiments were carried out on a number of workers, but he focused the most on a Dutch immigrant he referred to as "Schmidt". Schmidt was monitored as he worked and rested, and Taylor measured the exact time of every move Schmidt made: everything was quantified. Taylor believed that there was significant room for improvement of Schmidt's productivity, and following Taylor's instructions Schmidt was able to shovel 47 tons of pig iron in the same amount of time that he earlier used to shovel 12.5 tons. Of course, the increase in productivity took more of an effort from Schmidt, and Taylor believed that he would have to be compensated if he was to put in more of an effort, but it only took a 40 per cent rise in his wages to increase his productivity by nearly 400 per cent. For Taylor this was positive proof of the validity of his theory of scientific management.

Taylor described Schmidt as an extremely stupid individual, and he saw this as a major advantage ([1911] 2007: 36–9). In his theory, the manual worker should only provide the muscles, whereas management should do all the thinking. The labour process itself became completely detached from the skills of the worker; there is no hint of craftsmanship or tradition left in the daily tasks of the worker, who ideally should be as mindless as a robot. Because all knowledge and initiative on the workers' part is factored out, management has virtually complete control of the entire labour process. A worker who attempted to think or suggest a different way of doing anything would simply be regarded as out of order. It is hardly an exaggeration to call this degrading. In order to get the workers to accept such a regimen at work, Taylor believed that one would have to raise their wages, but he also saw that a measure of force would be necessary.

The most successful implementation of Taylorist principles was in the Ford Motor Company, where it was combined with the use of assembly lines. The basic technology of assembly lines was already in use, for example, in the meat industry, but Ford changed the way the technology was utilized. The basic idea of an assembly line is that rather than bringing the worker to the work, the work is brought to the worker, who remains stationary. As a result, management can determine the speed at which any given task is to be completed and the principle of the division of labour is taken to a completely new level. The workers who assembled the cars for Ford needed very little skill, and it was seen as an advantage if they in fact had virtually no skill or capacity for thought; all skill and thought was placed with management. In an interview with the *Chicago Tribune* in 1916, Ford declared: "History is more or less bunk. It's tradition. We don't want tradition. We want to live in the present, and the only history that is worth a tinker's damn is the history that we make today." The organization of labour in his factories was fully in accordance with this as no shred of history and tradition was left in the labour process. The work was characterized by mind-numbing monotony, but Ford believed that the workers would be more than willing to accept such "degradation" if they were only paid sufficiently high wages.

Work at the assembly line was not quite as insane as portrayed in Charlie Chaplin's film *Modern Times* (1936), but the parody definitely hit its mark. In the Fordist paradigm, the worker was more or less regarded as a mechanical part of the machine. This was brilliantly depicted in Chaplin's film when he is sucked into the machinery and merges with it. His convulsive twitches show how the temporality of the machine has possessed the human body. There is also a bizarre scene where poor Chaplin is strapped into an automatic feeding machine. When the worker is given nutrition, he will be able to continue working; it is no different from providing an engine with fuel.

In 1940 the Ford Motor Company produced a short film of its own, *Symphony in F*, which can be regarded as a response to Chaplin's *Modern Times*. It attempted to convey a more positive image of work at the assembly line. The pace is slow, highlighting the beauty of how everything comes together, showing just a few repetitions of every single operation, so that little or none of the monotony comes across. Finally the entire factory is turned into a magic kingdom where all the car parts are animated and the cars actually build themselves. The film ends with the words: "From the earth come the materials to be transformed for human service by Ford men, management and machines." Chaplin's grotesque portrayal of life at the assembly line was probably far closer to the truth, which is why the Ford Motor Company had to increase their wages so dramatically.

Before the Ford Motor Company introduced the famous $5 day, the turnover rate was 370 per cent, which means that the entire workforce had to be replaced almost four times a year. The main reason for the high turnover was not that people got fired; they resigned because they could not stand the work, despite the financial hardships the average worker faced. At Ford, the $5 day seemed to make the monotony more bearable. After all, the average weekly income at this time was $11. The *Wall Street Journal* dismissed the $5 day as "foolish", whereas the *New York Evening Post* described it as "a magnificent act of generosity". They were both wrong, and Ford himself described it as a brilliant cost-cutting move. The assembly line lead to such an increase in productivity that Ford could have afforded to pay his workers four times as much, $20 a day, while making the same profits as he used to.

The ideal of the Fordist production model was the completely inflexible worker who performs exactly the same, optimized operation time after time. The workers stayed in one place and the machinery moved. A problem with that approach is that employers often got more inflexibility from the workers than they wanted. Deskilled workers who found little satisfaction in their work except for the wages became more and more hostile and uncooperative towards their employers. They became reluctant to perform any tasks that were not explicitly mentioned in the job description, and everything became a question of bargaining. Even sabotage was not uncommon; it should probably be seen as a moral protest against the working conditions and as a way of demonstrating the workers' autonomy in a factory system that would grant them none.

Immanuel Kant's moral philosophy can help us see what is morally questionable in such an organization of labour. From a Kantian perspective, all humans – even workers – should be treated as ends in themselves. He writes: "So act that you use humanity, whether in your own person or in the person of any other, always at the same time as an end and never merely as a means" (Kant [1785] 1998: 38). Essentially this means having respect for persons. Kant claims that if we treat human beings as mere tools with no value apart from this, we pay them no respect. It should be noted that Kant does not say that we cannot in any way use people as means to our ends. Whenever we pay someone to provide us with goods of some sort, in effect we are using that person as a means to an end. Kant's point is that one should not treat a human being *merely* as a means, but always also as an end in itself. What is more, we must respect what makes that being *human*, that is, his or her capacity for autonomous or self-directed behaviour. It is patently obvious that Taylor's model for scientific management and its implementation at Ford's factories had no room for the workers' autonomy. From a Kantian perspective, it must be described as immoral.

Taylorism appears to be a clear example of the evils of production under capitalism, as described by Marx. In 1913, Lenin's view of Taylor's theory of scientific management was absolutely dismissive; he described it as an attempt "to squeeze out of the worker three times more labour during a working day of the same length as before" (Lenin [1913] 1968: 594). But his attitude had undergone radical change the next year, when he wrote:

The Taylor system – without its initiators knowing or wishing it – is preparing the time when the proletariat will take over

all social production and appoint its own workers' commit-
tees for the purpose of properly distributing and rationalising
all social labour.   (Lenin [1914] 1968: 154)

Lenin grew firmer in this conviction over the following years, and
by 1918 he believed that the Russian Revolution could not succeed
without Taylorism. Lenin's intentions differed from Taylor's because
Lenin did not want to increase the profits of the capitalists, but
rather use increased labour efficiency to reduce working hours,
which is close to the ideal presented by Marx in the third volume of
Capital. The younger Marx, however, would probably have accused
Lenin of subjecting workers to the worst form of alienation. Indeed,
an anti-Taylor faction called "left Communism" emerged within the
Communist Party, but they were dismissed by Lenin as suffering
from "an infantile disorder" ([1920] 2001). Stalin shared Lenin's
belief, arguing that: "The combination of the Russian revolutionary
sweep with American efficiency is the essence of Leninism" (quoted
in Hughes 2004: 251). Taylorism was never fully implemented in the
Soviet factories, and in 1935 a more homegrown variety of scientific management, the so-called Stakhanovite movement, began.
The Soviet authorities reported astonishing increases in productivity caused by the movement, but these reports were later shown
to be mainly fiction; the movement did increase productivity, but
to a far lesser extent than Taylorism. What is more, it was hardly
any less "alienating" than Taylorism.

    Both Taylor's theory of scientific management and its Russian
variant were designed for the industrial worker. As the twentieth
century progressed and the industrial society was replaced by
the post-industrial society, that kind of worker became increasingly atypical. The post-industrial economy has fewer blue-collar
jobs and more white-collar jobs. In the 1950s white-collar workers
already outnumbered blue-collar workers in the USA, and today 80
per cent of US workers are categorized as white-collar. The blue-

collar or industrial worker will not disappear, just as the farmer did not disappear when we left the agricultural society, but will become an increasingly marginal figure in work life as a whole. "White-collar worker" is a broad term. If we narrow it down and look at people whose job primarily consists in handling information, that is, "knowledge workers", they now make up more than half of the American workforce. If there is such a thing as a "typical" worker in our society, that person spends most of his or her time handling information. A problem with referring to certain types of workers as "knowledge workers" is that it seems to imply that knowledge is not essential to others kinds of work, which is of course nonsense. Such an understanding seems to be based on an extremely narrow and intellectualist conception of knowledge. Aristotle pointed out that there are various form of knowledge, some more theoretical and others more practical, and practical knowledge is also knowledge. We tend to misrepresent the amount of knowledge it actually takes to perform manual labour well. The difference between intellectual and manual labour is one of degree, not an absolute distinction; all jobs will have both aspects.

As the character of work has changed, so has management. There has for instance been increasing emphasis on so-called "soft skills", which refer to what sort of *person* one is – if you are sociable, cooperative and so on – in contrast to "hard skills", which denote technical competence. One reason why "soft skills" have risen to such prominence is that teamwork is more common. Teams tend to be short-lived because they are usually formed with a specific project in mind; when that project is finished the team is usually disbanded and the individual members move on to new teams and new projects. As fully functioning team workers, we must be able to work together with a constantly changing group of co-workers as we move from team to team. We carry with us skills that are supposed to be immediately applicable in a new team. The basic model is more like serial monogamy than a marriage.

With the "knowledge worker" the discipline of "knowledge management" also emerged. The main idea behind knowledge management is that workers should transfer their knowledge to the corporate database such that the corporation in turn could transmit this knowledge to other employees. This is a modern variety of Taylor's theory of scientific management. The only difference is that it is now applied to the knowledge worker and not only the manual worker. Taylor described how managers would take on "the burden of gathering together all of the traditional knowledge which in the past has been possessed by the workmen and then of classifying, tabulating, and reducing this knowledge to rules, laws, and formulae" (Taylor [1911] 2007: 24). Knowledge management is an application of this principle to a new domain. This is completely in accordance with Taylor's own beliefs, as he believed that his scientific management should be applied to all sorts of work, including managing government and universities. The underlying idea is that knowledge can be stored and passed on to those who do not have it, and further that it is a commodity with a value.

All workers apparently have to be "managed" in order to ensure that they are doing what they are supposed to be doing. In Chaplin's *Modern Times*, the president of the company has surveillance cameras installed all over the factory, and can observe all the workers, whereas they cannot observe him. He even watches the bathrooms. Jeremy Bentham's idea of a Panopticon easily comes to mind here. It was a prison building designed such that a guard could observe all the prisoners without the prisoners being able to tell whether or not they were being observed. The essential idea is that the prisoner could never be certain if he was actually being watched, and he would therefore behave "properly". Bentham himself described it as a "new mode of obtaining power of mind over mind, in a quantity hitherto without example" (Bentham [1787] 1995: 31).

Controlling the workers has been an essential aspect of management theories from their inception. The emphasis on control indicates that the employer and the employee do not share a common interest. If they had a shared interest, the need for control would be considerably reduced. Particularly in many jobs at the bottom of the corporate ladder – especially so-called McJobs – Taylorist principles are still operative. What about workers higher up the corporate hierarchy? Today they are under closer surveillance than at any time in history. The latest incarnation of Taylorism is so-called "enterprise systems". What Taylor did for the blue-collars, they do for white-collar workers in attempting to standardize and increase efficiency in all tasks. Employees are supposed to follow given procedures, and management will usually set the pace. It is a post-industrial version of Ford's production lines. This can be see in few places as clearly as in call centres, where the employees must follow standardized scripts and only spend a given amount of time on each call. Using computer technology, management can monitor what employees do all day, how great their output is and so on. There is a fairly clear line from current enterprise systems back to Taylor's and Ford's ideals.

Many executives are constantly shopping for new "philosophies". Sometimes this is mainly a change of words – such as talking about "leadership" rather than "management" – and sometimes it is about introducing something that is supposed to transform the entire organization. The general impression I get from much current management literature is that it is a version of the counter-cultural slogans of the 1960s and 1970s: freedom, individuality and imagination. It is all the old hippie clichés, but now in a corporate setting. We are supposed to be non-conformist, original, independent, creative and playful, while at the same time being a "team player". We should be strong, but also be in touch with our emotions and develop our "soft skills". These qualities can be pretty hard to combine. In the television series *The Office*, manager David Brent seems to have stumbled on the truth, when he says: "Team playing. I call it 'team individuality'. It's a new ... It's like a management style. Again, guilty, unorthodox – sue me" (Gervais & Merchant 2003).

The contemporary leader is supposed to convince the employee that his job is not merely a job, but rather a fantastic opportunity for realizing his full potential, for him to become his "true self". Genuine leadership is allegedly about putting the human as a whole at the centre. Self-realization at work is about "upgrading" oneself in a way that goes well beyond one's professional skills: one's entire self is up for improvement. The employee is underdeveloped as a person, and is supposed to overcome this deficiency through work. He or she – and the entire organization as well – is in a constant process of learning, and this is an aspect of work that goes beyond getting paid. It is all about becoming who he or she can be. Contrary to the Taylorist model of leadership, the leader will not *force* anyone to do anything, but will rather motivate employees to transform themselves in ways that are also desirable for the organization. Companies should now utilize employees' own propensities, their own search for personal fulfilment, rather than work against them or assume that their propensities and the interests of the company are fundamentally at odds with each other. The motives and goals of the employee and the organization are supposed to be in perfect harmony. Management passes through the soul of each and every employee. Instead of imposing discipline on workers from the outside, new management motivates them from the inside.

The worker in the Fordist paradigm had no soul, whereas the worker in much contemporary management theory is all soul. One is now supposed to internalize the corporate culture, and embody the company's values and "spirit". Compared to the Fordist paradigm, where the worker was regarded more or less as an automaton, the turn in management theory towards the worker as a being with thoughts and feelings was an improvement, but sometimes contemporary management strategies seem more appropriate for a cult than for a "normal" company. Among the spookiest books I have ever read is Jesper Kunde's *Corporate Religion* (2000). It would almost be more attractive to suddenly find yourself in one of fantasy writer H. P. Lovecraft's horror stories than to actually work in a company governed by Kunde's principles! The basic idea is that you must *believe* in your brand, and we are not simply talking about thinking that you are working with a good product. The belief in question is a total faith in "the corporate soul". The areas of management, human resources, corporate culture and branding are all supposed to be brought together in a holy unity. The customers are ordinary "believers", the employees are "missionaries" and the CEO is the "spiritual leader". Kunde himself is probably the Messiah.

Looking on the shelves devoted to "leadership" in a book shop, we can find such "gems" as David Baron and Lynette Padwa's *Moses on Management: 50 Leadership Lessons from the Greatest Manager of All Time*, Robert Dilenschneider's *Moses: CEO: Lessons in Leadership*, Laurie Beth Jones's *Jesus CEO: Using Ancient Wisdom for Visionary Leadership* and Stefan Rudnicki's *Confucius in the Boardroom: Ancient Wisdom, Modern Lessons for Business*. If we find those too "spiritual", we might prefer a more literary approach, such as Norman Augustine and Kenneth Adelman's *Shakespeare in Charge: The Bard's Guide to Leading and Succeeding on the Business Stage* or John Whitney and Tina Packer's *Power Plays: Shakespeare's Lessons in Leadership and Management*. If Shakespeare is too highbrow, we could always go for Gloria Gilbert Mayer and Thomas Mayer's *Goldilocks on Management*. Then there are books that use "tough guy" as ideals, such as Deborrah Himsel's *Leadership Sopranos Style* and Anthony Schneider's *Tony Soprano on Management*. Among the weirdest titles I found was Wess Roberts's *Leadership Secrets of Attila the Hun* and its sequel *Victory Secrets of Attila the Hun*. I definitely do not want a boss who takes leadership advice from Attila the Hun! Such a leader would confirm the so-called Peter Principle: "In a hierarchy every employee tends to rise to his level of incompetence".

I occasionally give overpaid lectures to the business community. In order to prepare for these lectures, I read a few of the most popular current books on management, not because I talk much about management myself, but rather because I wish to know what sorts of ideas are currently in circulation among the audience. The "substance" of these books tends to be somewhat underwhelming. They usually consist of a handful of catchy headlines and a multitude of examples – or "cases" – that are supposed to back up the broad generalizations in the headlines. The claims are often referred to as a "philosophy", although they fall short of what philosophers tend to regard as philosophy. The fact that bad books exist is not much of a problem in itself, but these books have real impact on people's lives, far more than what "proper" philosophy books tend to have. For instance, when "downsizing" became the mantra of the day in the 1990s, as cutting down the company to bare essentials was supposed to maximize profits for shareholders, the result was that a lot of people lost their jobs. It turned out that this approach had been far too heavy-handed, so "downsizing" was followed by "rightsizing", which meant that many of the jobs that had been cut were reintroduced.

These books on management have a tendency to fall short in their predictions. One of the most successful books in this genre has been Tom Peters's *In Search of Excellence* (1982). Five years after the publication of the book, it turned out that the companies he had described as "excellent" did significantly worse than those he had described as seriously lacking in "excellence". Satisfying Peters's six "measures of excellence" was a great recipe for being a loser in the market. The fact that following the advice given in such books does not seem to be of any help, but on the contrary may have the opposite effect, has not had any impact on the popularity of the genre.

One of the leading management gurus of the twentieth century, Peter Drucker, correctly pointed out: "So much of what we call management consists in making it difficult for people to work". Being "managed" can be awfully time-consuming and frustrating.

One of the main reasons why *The Office*'s David Brent is one of the worst managers conceivable is that – in addition to his narcissism, bigotry, lack of social skills and terrible sense of humour – he has read or taken a quick glance at a number of books on management. They clearly further corrupted his already abysmally poor judgement. The episode in which he attempts to be a motivational speaker, starting by playing Tina Turner's "Simply the Best" on his CD-player, is one of the most hilarious – and painful – moments in television history.

I am not arguing that all theories of management are bad, but it is hard to avoid a certain queasiness when reading much of the cheesier stuff that currently poses as a "management philosophy". Apparently, *fun* is the happening thing at the moment. Just when we thought that business literature could get no lower, various books about how to have and why to have fun at work have appeared. Among them we find Dave Hemsath and Leslie Yerkes's *301 Ways to Have Fun at Work* and Matt Weinstein's *Managing to Have Fun: How Fun at Work Can Motivate Your Employees, Inspire Your Coworkers, and Boost Your Bottom Line*. And if we thought that what passed as management consulting could not possible get more ridiculous, we would be amazed by the appearance of "funsultants" and "funcilitators". Of course work can be fun – it often is – but the fun tends to emerge spontaneously. Mandatory or enforced fun simply is not fun. Some years ago, I was involved in a project that was supposed to lead to the creation of a website for futurology, that is, studies of the future. A number of competent people were involved, and we were willing to do the work for free because it sounded like great fun. Unfortunately, the leader of the project took the idea of having fun too literally, so we spent all our time "playing", and being "creative", without any clear plan for what all this "creativity" was supposed to lead to. After having been a part of this project for a year, in which we had "played" a lot, but not actually *done* anything, I left. All play and no work made

Lars a bored boy. Any executive who is tempted to enforce a new regime of fun at work, should be forced to watch all episodes of *The Office*, and hopefully come to an understanding of why that is a terrible idea. David Brent says: "You will never have another boss like me. Someone who's basically a chilled out entertainer" (Gervais & Merchant 2003). Having a boss who constantly attempts to entertain us is mental torture. Treating employees as adults rather than as children in need of entertainment is a much better idea than becoming an incarnation of David Brent.

Being "managed" can be one of the most frustrating features of one's professional life. If I were to make a guess, I would think that the emphasis on management – or some of its equivalents, such as "leadership" – will continue to haunt the contemporary workplace and probably even increase. There is little the average employee can do about this, except to pretend to listen, maybe get a sensible word in every now and then and wait for the management fad to pass before it is replaced by another one.

6. Getting paid

How much would you like to get paid? The obvious answer seems to be: as much as possible. Virtually everyone would prefer a higher wage over a lower one because we assume that in some sense we would be more satisfied with a higher wage. Research on happiness – or subjective well-being as it is commonly called in such studies – indicates that this relation between a higher wage and a higher level of satisfaction is far from obvious (cf. Lane 2000: 59–76). There seems to be a fairly clear relation between these factors in poor societies, but as societies get richer, this relation between levels of income and satisfaction becomes weaker. In the richest societies, there is hardly any relation between the two at all, except for the very poorest people in those societies. There are some studies that indicate a slight increase in happiness with higher income, but it makes virtually no impact compared to other factors, such as health and personal relationships. This holds for both the rich and those with moderate incomes in rich societies. It is clearly a case of diminishing returns: the more you make, the less difference additional income will make.

Habituation also plays a significant role here. As a student, I managed on £7,000–£8,000 a year. That was sufficient for rent, clothes, books, food, alcohol and cigarettes. When I became a research fellow on a scholarship, I suddenly made nearly £25,000 a year, and for the first couple of months I felt that I was virtually swimming in money; that did not last long, and I became accustomed to that level of income pretty quickly. Today I simply cannot understand how I possibly made ends meet. Were I suddenly to make two or three times as much as I do today, I am sure that my present level of income would soon appear to be ridiculously insufficient. We get used to a higher level of income pretty quickly and forget the improvement we have had. Am I happier today than I was when I was living on £7,000–£8,000 a year? I doubt it. Would I be much happier if I started making two or three times as much as I do today? I doubt that as well.

Most people believe that they would become significantly happier if they had a 25 per cent increase in their wages. However, if we compare a person with a median income in a rich country with another person who makes 25 per cent more, the person who makes more will on average not be any happier. So if we are aiming for happiness, we probably should not put much emphasis on making more money, and we should definitely not give it a higher priority than maintaining a good relationship with our family and friends.

How important are your wages for you? Is the net amount of money you make the most important factor, or is it how much you make compared to other people? Imagine that you can choose between two hypothetical worlds:

(1)   You make £35,000 annually and others make £45,000.
(2)   You make £25,000 annually and others make £20,000.

We further assume that all other conditions are equal, such that you would have £10,000 more to spend on goods in world (1) in addition to those goods you could have purchased for your £25,000 in world (2). Which world would you choose? According to standard economic theory, world (1) is the obvious answer because it gives you the greatest purchasing power, but a high number of people answer that they would prefer to live in world (2). This shows that many people would be willing to give up a substantial amount of their absolute income in order to improve their relative income.

How much we get paid *compared to others* is clearly of importance to us. It says something about our social position, our *value* in the social hierarchy. Generally, those who receive money for their time are held in higher esteem than those whose time is "free", such as pensioners and housewives. There are exceptions to this: drug pushers and prostitutes, for example, are not usually held in higher esteem than pensioners. There seems to be no clear relation between esteem and monetary compensation in the case of religious leaders, except for the occasional inverse relationship, where religion as big business can be a pretty distasteful phenomenon. Apart from such exceptions, there seems to be some perceived connection between what people charge for their time and their perceived "worth". We can, of course, dismiss such a perceived connection as utter nonsense – and we should – but it is nevertheless a feature of the social hierarchies of our culture. The supposition seems to be that if your time has greater (economic) value than other people's time, then you must also be a more valuable person.

Getting paid is central to our idea of work. We will often distinguish between work and a hobby because one of them is paid and the other is not, even though they can take the same amount of physical and mental effort. People who do something for free, for purely idealistic reasons, tend to become *less* satisfied if they start getting paid. One would expect the opposite. After all, if you continue to do something you like, but also get paid to do it, you presumably have a good deal. The problem is that it changes one's relation to the activity itself. It transforms an inherently meaningful activity into a poorly paid job. In that sense, one should probably be careful not to make one's biggest interest into a job, but rather go for something slightly less interesting, and leave the main interest "unspoiled" by money. I am speaking from experience here: when philosophy became my job, the personal satisfaction I felt from doing it dropped considerably. Fortunately, I found new hobbies.

Even though getting paid is a central feature of our notion of work, one can hardly regard it as a necessary criterion of work, simply because there is clearly such a thing as unpaid work. It would be strange to claim that slaves do not work. Slavery has been the rule rather than the exception in human history. It is estimated that four out of five advanced agricultural societies have been based on some form of slave labour. A significant part of the African population – at least a third – was enslaved even before the atrocious European and American slave trade began, and the economies of ancient Greece and Rome were founded on slavery. The institution of slavery was generally accepted in the ancient world, but there were some philosophers, like the Sophists, who raised their objections to the practice. Alcidamas, a pupil of Gorgias, is said to have argued: "God has set all men free – nature has made no man a slave". However, this was a minority opinion, and mainstream philosophy accepted and defended slavery. The slaves were usually treated quite humanely by the Greeks and the Romans, at least compared to the horrors that befell the Africans who later were enslaved by Europeans and Americans, but they were nevertheless the property of others. In the Middle Ages, slavery was replaced by the institution of serfdom. It is not entirely clear how one should distinguish between the slave and the serf, and the Latin word *servus* is also the root for "slave". The serf had slightly more freedom than the slave. He was not a commodity that was bought and sold to the same extent, and he was more at liberty to decide how and when he would work, as long as he delivered what his lord was entitled to. Eventually the institution of serfdom also faded away, even though it took some time before it was abolished by law. The main reason for its demise was probably more economic than humanitarian: wage labour simply seemed to be more efficient. As Adam Smith put it: "From the experience of all ages and nations, I believe, that the work done by freemen comes cheaper in the end than the work performed by slaves" ([1776] 1981: 99). Smith also had a moral argument against slavery, and protested strongly against the cruelty of reducing people "into the vilest of all states, that of domestic slavery, and to sell them, man, woman, and child, like so many herds of cattle, to the highest bidder in the market" ([1759] 1982: 282). However, the economic argument seems to have made more of an impact than the moral.

Another reason why the relation between work and wages is contingent is simply that work is a much older phenomenon than money. What we immediately can recognize as work existed for thousands of years before money was invented. Agriculture is work. It is, of course, not easy to date the first instances of agriculture, but *systematic* agriculture goes back at least as far as 10,000 BCE in the areas we today refer to as southern Iraq and Syria, where farmers began to cultivate plants. (Some argue that the Peruvians were just as early, and started cultivating grain and squash before 10,000 BCE, but this is a matter of dispute.) And agricultural practices started to spread, first to Egypt, and then to India and China. By 5000 BCE, especially in Sumer, agricultural practices had become extremely sophisticated, and different workers specialized in their respective fields of competence: a division of labour was emerging.

The point is that all this should be regarded as work, even if the institution of money had not yet been invented. The invention of money was an extremely significant event, and some have even argued that the monetization of Greek society was a necessary condition for the invention of philosophy, because it fundamentally changed social relations and made possible ideas of an impersonal universe (cf. Seaford 2004). Gertrude Stein went a little bit too far when she claimed that "the thing that differentiates man from animals is money", but she had a point. Money was a necessary condition for creating a vast social nexus beyond what had been possible earlier. An important step in the development of money was when it was no longer used to pay only for objects, but also for work. That made work itself into a commodity. And more than that, it was the first step towards the modern evaluation of people's time in terms of money, leading up to Benjamin Franklin's statement: "Time is money" (1987: 320). This has been taken to the extreme by the British economics professor Ian Walker, who even made a formula for the monetary value of time: $V = (W((100 - t)/100))/C$, where V is the value of an hour, W is a person's hourly wage, t is the tax rate and C is the local cost of living. Using this formula he found that the average British minute is worth just over 10 pence to men and eight pence to women. As a result, brushing your teeth will cost you 30 pence, washing your car by hand will cost you £3 and you will probably save money by ordering a takeaway meal rather than cooking it yourself.

Today, we are so accustomed to the idea of wage labour that it seems strange that many workers rejected the very idea for a long time. Wage labour is so deeply engrained in our current societies that few people argue against it. When we look back to the Industrial Revolution, we see that the workers' resistance to wage labour was fierce. The historical background to this opposition was that craftsmen had been organized in guilds, and these guilds had quite a lot of power. When factories – where people were paid wages – were established, the power of the guilds was undermined. Only wealthy merchants could afford to set up factories and a large number of craftsmen who had been members of guilds could not compete with the factories, and chose to become paid employees, but they did so with great resentment. A major reason for this dislike of work in the factories was, of course, that it certainly was no picnic. Many factory owners handed out corporal punishment, especially to child labourers, while others settled for fines. One could be fined for idleness, looking out of a window, chatting with other workers and so on. There was very little room for slacking, and supervision was tight. What bothered the workers was not only the harsh treatment, but also the very fact that they were subjected to somebody else's will. They did not like being answerable to someone else who would pay them a given wage, and many compared it to slavery – as in the term "wage slave" – or prostitution.

Workers frequently argued that the difference between the worth of what they produced and what they were actually paid was money that was in effect stolen from them. Conflicts between employers and employees were often intense and sometimes violent. The conflicts eventually became more "civilized" and, rather than aiming for "total liberation", workers negotiated for higher wages, shorter hours, better working conditions and so on. They became less concerned with whether they received everything they were "due" – that is, if a surplus was "stolen" from them – and focused more on whether the wages they received were sufficient to support a family. This meant that workers accepted wage labour and the corresponding division of power. Contrary to the wishes of revolutionary Marxism, they no longer challenged the capitalist paradigm, but rather had the more modest ambition of improving their condition within that paradigm. It also meant that workers would invest more of their hope for freedom and personal fulfilment in their role as consumers. The major aim now became to increase the wages because that would lead to increased possibilities for consumption.

"Everyone but an idiot knows that the lower classes must be kept poor, or they will never be industrious", the English writer Arthur Young argued (Young 1771: 361). Whenever this is quoted one rarely includes Young's qualification of his claim: "I do not mean, that the poor of England must be kept like the poor of France, but, the state of the country considered, they must (like all mankind) be in poverty or they will not work." He was still wrong. Adam Smith was the first to move beyond the assumption of the necessity of poverty by formulating a theory of growth that contained rising real wages, because economic growth could in fact sustain higher wages. He argued that wages should at least be sufficient to sustain a family and provide for a tolerable life. In fact, he was probably the first to frame this in terms of social justice: "It is but equity, besides, that they who feed, cloath and lodge the whole body of the people, should have such a share of the produce of their own labour as to be themselves tolerably well fed, cloathed and lodged" (Smith [1776] 1981: 96). Smith's economic theory was motivated by his concern for the poor, and his moral defence of capitalism was that it was the system that in the long run would most improve conditions for workers. Marx shared Smith's concerns but, contrary to Smith, Marx believed that capitalism would necessarily lead to a decline in real wages. Smith was right and Marx was wrong. Contrary to Marx's predictions, real wages in the industrial society did not decline. In fact, they rose far faster than inflation, and they did so well before the introduction of minimum wages by governments.

How much should someone get paid? For the believer in the free market, the answer is simple: whatever the market is willing to pay. Socialists have come up with two different answers: some argue that workers should be paid in accordance with their contribution to society whereas others argue that people should be paid in accordance with their needs. Marx argued for both versions or, more precisely, he argued that in the initial stages of communist society one would have to accept the first version, but the goal was to end up with the second. In a famous passage from *Critique of the Gotha Programme*, Marx writes: "From each according to his abilites, to each according to his needs!" ([1875] 1996: 215). This might seem like a good idea; a 1987 poll even showed that almost half the population of the United States believed that the phrase stems from the US Constitution!

An obvious problem with this approach is that it is far from simple to determine what a person's *needs are*. One thing Marx mentions is the number of people one has to provide for. He does not mention people with disabilities, but would probably not have any problem with accepting that they can have greater needs than others. What is more, needs do not only depend on disabilities and the like, but also on social background. Somebody who has been brought up in a wealthy environment will usually have needs that are more expensive to satisfy than those of a person from a poor environment. Perceived needs can vary considerable from one person to the next. If one were to map out everybody's individual needs, this system would become extremely complicated. It might also appear to be quite unfair.

One can also settle for an intermediate position – the most common and probably the most reasonable – where everyone is guaranteed a certain level of income through wages or social services, but where inequalities in income, as determined by the market, are allowed. There will still be a question of what level the minimum standard should be, but I have no intention of addressing that here. This is a *meritocratic* system with a certain threshold below which nobody is supposed to fall. Most people seem to share an intuition that a meritocratic order is fair, because people should receive different incomes depending on their contribution.

This leads us back to a point we discussed at the beginning of the chapter. How much we get paid compared to others appears to be of importance to us because it says something about our "value" in the social hierarchy. However, we also saw that an increase in wages is unlikely to improve our happiness much, unless we happen to be at the very bottom of the pay scale. If we are unhappy with what we are currently making, we are unlikely to get much happier if we start making more. Getting promoted is a part of the same phenomenon. If we are promoted, that seems to indicate something about our worth. But will a promotion make us happier? If someone wants a promotion and gets it, one would assume that they become more satisfied. Surprisingly, the opposite seems to be the case: workers who have recently been promoted tend to become *less* satisfied. The problem is that a promotion will often lead to the expectation of further promotions. Even if we have improved our absolute position, we will tend to become less satisfied with our relative position.

Perhaps, then, we should avoid promotions. A friend of mine has chosen this approach. He works as a warehouseman, at the very bottom of the corporate ladder, and even though his manager repeatedly has attempted to make him foreman, he has constantly refused to move up in the hierarchy – even threatening to hand in his resignation – since all he wants is a simple job with limited responsibilities, and then he can focus on all the other things he enjoys in life, such as being with friends, writing short stories and making music.

I am not convinced that his approach is the right one, either. He has an instrumentalist view of work, and regards it merely as something he does in order to make living. From such a perspective, work has no inherent value, and is good only in terms of the income it brings. But our relation to work can never be exclusively instrumental because it forms us as persons and is part of the expression of who we are. What you do for many hours a day year after year will necessarily shape you as a person. Shouldn't something you spend that much of your life on be something that in some sense *matters* to you? Work clearly seems to satisfy more needs than the merely pecuniary. The role it plays in providing our lives with *meaning* is more fundamental. In several big surveys in different countries, most people state that they would continue to work even if they had enough money to set them up for life, without having to work another day. It is fairly common among lottery winners to keep working, even though they do not have to do so for financial reasons. Work seems to fill an existential need, rather than only being a source of income. Samuel Johnson was therefore probably not right when he stated: "Every man is, or hopes to be, an idler" (Johnson [1758] 2003: 407). Of course, virtually everybody thinks from time to time of how wonderful it would be to be set up financially for life, not having to work another day, but then what would one fill one's life with?

7. Work in an age of affluence

John Maynard Keynes wrote in 1930 that nobody will "look forward to the age of leisure and abundance without a dread" ([1930] 1963: 358). To a great extent we now live in that "dreaded" age. However, the age of abundance and the age of leisure have not been realized to an equal extent: abundance has increased far more than leisure.

Productivity levels increased significantly after the Second World War: in fact, they more than doubled. In principle that means that we could have the same standard of living as people fifty years ago, but only work half as much as the average worker back then. The point is, if you are satisfied with a given material standard of living, never wanting to raise it above that level, the increase in productivity will provide you with more and more time for leisure. But rather than exploiting the increase in productivity for more leisure, we have chosen to raise our standard of living, becoming – seen from the perspective of earlier societies – ridiculously affluent. The average reader of this book is better off in terms of material wealth than more than 99 per cent of the people who have ever lived. Most kings and queens of earlier days would be envious of your level of material wealth. Of course, it will not seem like that for you in your everyday life, but that is simply because you take this standard of living for granted.

We have chosen shopping over leisure. People used to have different priorities. There is solid evidence from pre-modern times and early modernity that higher wages led people to work less. Even well into the industrial age employers frequently found that many workers were absent for the first few days after wages had been paid. "Extra money", that is, money beyond what was needed to pay for the basic necessities of life, was often spent on taking time off work rather than on increasing one's material wealth. Our priorities have changed since then.

In the 1950s John Kenneth Galbraith coined the expression "affluent society" (Galbraith 1958). It should be noted that he used it partly ironically to describe a society that is rich in private resources and poor in public ones. He was critical of the growth in private consumption, and argued that the state should rather guide resources towards the improvement of social services, schools and so on: it should shrink the private sector significantly and increase the public sector. The criticism of consumption follows in the path of Thorstein Veblen's classic *The Theory of the Leisure Class* (1899), but there is an essential difference. Veblen described the effects of prosperity on the few, on the very rich, whereas Galbraith described a society characterized by *mass* prosperity. Even though Galbraith's "cure" does not appear to be economically sound, his claim that mass prosperity would have enormous consequences for the very fabric of society could hardly have been more accurate.

The expression "affluent society" no longer seems to carry any of its ironic meaning: the affluent society has become a reality. As Brink Lindsay points out in *The Age of Abundance* (2007), his excellent study of American politics and culture in the post-war era, the most important cultural shift in this period has been the move from scarcity to abundance. Very few people in the West have to struggle for their survival, and instead they search frantically for their identity. Consumption is an essential part of this. In the age of affluence, workers no longer dream of overthrowing the bourgeoisie, but rather settle for joining it. They no longer yearn for control of the means of production, and rather concentrate on increasing their means for consumption.

It has also meant that an essential aspect of the Protestant work ethic has been left behind: the idea of delayed gratification.

According to the Protestant ethic we are supposed to work hard and then later reap what we have sown. As Sennett points out, the short-term perspective of the new capitalism "makes nonsense of delayed gratification as a principle of self-discipline" (2006: 78). The institutional conditions that gave meaning to the idea are no longer there. If everything in our work life is based on short-term perspectives, then so will be our expectation of gratification. We want *immediate* compensation for what we put in.

The idea of delayed gratification makes more sense in a religious context, with an idea of an afterlife, than in a context where this earthly existence is all we have. After all, we may not live to see the future where all the hard work is supposed to pay off. A car may hit me just before I am going to reap what I have sown. Or I may suffer the same fate as James Fixx, author of *The Complete Book of Running* (1977) and guru of the jogging boom, who died at the age of 52 of a massive heart attack after his daily run. We have no guarantee that the gratification will ever be ours. Exactly how long should we wait?

In the Pet Shop Boys song "To Step Aside", Neil Tennant sings about workers queuing, waiting for market forces to provide "a different kind of fate/Than to labour long and always wait" (Tennant & Lowe 1996). Tennant wrote these lines as he watched Hungarian workers from his window when he visited their country. It is interesting that the idea of delayed gratification was as essential to capitalist as to communist regimes. In both cases there was a promise of a future condition in which all hard work would be rewarded. As capitalism developed further, the delay of gratification became shorter and shorter, whereas it seemed to be increased in the dysfunctional communist economies. The differences were patently clear in 1959, when Vice-President Richard Nixon visited Soviet Premier Nikita Khrushchev in Moscow for the US National Exhibition, in the midst of the Cold War. Brink Lindsay tells the story of this historical encounter in *The Age of Abundance*, quoting Nixon's claim that "the United States, the world's largest capitalist country, has from the standpoint of distribution of wealth come closest to the ideal of prosperity for all in a classless society" (2007: 17). Nixon, the pathological liar, was actually telling the truth. The centrepiece of the exhibition in Moscow was a six-room ranch house. The Soviet press referred to the house as "Taj Mahal", meaning that it was about as representative of life in the US as the Taj Mahal was for life in India. In fact, the house was priced at $14,000, which an ordinary American steel-worker could afford with a 30-year mortgage. Prosperity has picked up even greater speed since then.

Marx predicted that the working class would be increasingly impoverished under capitalism and that the standard of living would decline accordingly. It is obvious – for anyone not blinded by ideology – that exactly the opposite has happened. The end of the twentieth century and the beginning of the twenty-first have been characterized by extreme economic growth. As a result virtually everybody, both workers and capitalists, are significantly better off than they were only recently. However, capitalists have gained a significantly higher share of the growth than workers have. Profits have risen far faster than wages, which means that the relative share of workers has declined. This especially holds for so-called "unskilled" workers, who have actually suffered a relative loss in these years compared to the owners of businesses. However, those who are worse off, that is, those who have suffered this relative loss of wealth, are still in fact far better off in absolute figures than they were quite recently.

Another thing that should be kept in mind is that "the poor" is not a static category. Very few people in Western countries stay in that category permanently. For instance, the University of Michigan's Panel Survey on Income Dynamics showed that for the years 1975–91, only 0.5 per cent of the sample remained in the bottom quintile every year and only 5.1 per cent of those who were there in 1975 were still to be found there in 1991. There are also a large number of other studies that present a similar picture. Poverty is usually a temporary phenomenon for people in the Western world.

This fact is usually left out of the picture in books such as Polly Toynbee's account of life in low-pay Britain, *Hard Work* (2003), and Barbara Ehrenreich's *Nickel and Dimed* (2001), which chronicles her journey from one minimum wage job to another. The authors of such books usually only spend a few weeks, sometimes only a few days, with each employer before they move on to another equally miserable job. They find it impossible to make ends meet on the money they make. It is a heartbreaking picture of people living in highly undesirable conditions, and it is implied that the people who do these jobs are stuck there. But the "careers" Toynbee and Ehrenreich chronicle are highly untypical. Most people who start with very poorly paid jobs climb the economic ladder quite quickly, often within months. If Ehrenreich and Toynbee had chosen to extend their "excursions" to low-paid jobs and stayed longer, they would typically have increased their earnings pretty quickly. Of course, that would have spoiled the story they wanted to tell. It goes without saying that minimum wages are very low and that living on minimum wage is an ordeal, but one should also note that less than 2 per cent of Americans work for minimum wage and that half of those are under the age of 25. Very few people work for minimum wage for a long time. I certainly will not dispute that living on minimum wage must be very hard, but it is usually a temporary condition.

My point is not that those on the bottom do not have to endure hardship, but one should present a more nuanced picture than the one we are often given. There *is* reason for concern about the development we have seen in the past few decades, where growth in real income for the poor has been slow, well below the growth in income for those of average wealth, who in turn have had significantly slower growth than the already wealthy. This has consequences for the relative wealth of the poor. Herbert Spencer diagnosed the problem as early as in 1882:

Even those who are not directly spurred on by this intensified struggle for wealth and honour, are indirectly spurred on by it. For one of its effects is to raise the standard of living, and eventually to increase the average rate of expenditure for all. Partly for personal enjoyment, but much more for the display which brings admiration, those who acquire fortunes distinguish themselves by luxurious habits. The more numerous they become, the keener becomes the competition for that kind of public attention given to those who make themselves conspicuous by great expenditure. The competition spreads downwards step by step; until, to be "respectable," those having relatively small means feel obliged to spend more on houses, furniture, dress, and food; and are obliged to work the harder to get the requisite larger income.   (Spencer 1891: 488–9)

The problem is that many goods are positional, and one could even argue that all goods in some sense are positional. The utility of a positional good depends on how it compares with other goods of a similar type. If you have bought a new DVD player, and I then show you my Blu-ray player, the value of your player is diminished by the fact that mine is better. The same holds if I buy a four-room flat, and you then show me your new five-room flat, because the positional value of my flat is then diminished. The reason for this devaluation is that the context of evaluation changes. Even though the poor have in fact had a significant gain in material wealth, they may nevertheless have suffered a relative loss because others have had a higher increase, acquiring goods with a higher positional value. Goods are socially encoded, and the social context will determine what the necessities of life are. Adam Smith made this perfectly clear: "By necessaries I understand not only the commodities which are indispensably necessary for the support of life, but whatever the custom of the country renders it indecent for creditable people, even of the lowest order, to be without" (Smith [1776] 1981: 869–70). As the standards are raised for what counts as necessities, someone can fall further behind even if he or she has an absolute increase in their material wealth.

Even though growth in the past fifty years has been truly remarkable, there are clouds on the horizon. The essential feature of the age of affluence has been that prices have decreased and wages increased. This is as it should be according to standard economic theory: an increase in productivity makes goods and services cheaper, which means that people can buy more of them with their income, which in turn stimulates employment and generates higher wages, which in turn makes it possible for people to consume even more, and so on. It is a beneficial nexus of causes and effects, and it has worked beautifully. If this simple model were the whole truth, we would not see what we do today; namely, that working people are getting deeper and deeper into debt. Why is that? If prices go down and wages up, we should in principle be saving money, not getting into debt. The answer to the question as to why we accumulate more and more debt does not lie in our wages, but in our spending. Households that saved 10 per cent of their income only two decades ago, save nothing today. Even if our incomes have increased, our spending has increased a lot faster. Not saving is one thing, but living on credit is another. A major problem today is that many people spend well above their level of income. Living on credit is the current version of self-inflicted enslavement. Most people immediately think of the debts US consumers have accumulated, and they are certainly substantial, but the average Brit also spends well above his or her annual income. This has been great for the economy so far and contributed to the creation of many jobs, but it is also obvious that it cannot go on indefinitely.

The affluent society is a consumer society. This appears to have wide-ranging consequences for our relation to work. In a consumer society, our social status will not depend on our ability to produce something, but rather on our ability to consume it.

More and more people argue that consumption, not work, is the essential ingredient in the formation of social identity. The idea of consumption as essential to the formation of identity is fairly new. One cannot find much on the topic in the writings of for instance Smith and Marx. Marx's theory of the formation of identity was that productive work constitutes the human self: we are what we produce. In the consumer society we are what we consume. G. W. F. Hegel saw this possibility. According to Hegel, we express ourselves through work as we attach our will to external objects and thereby realize ourselves. Hegel also believed that this could be achieved by acquiring possessions. Buying an object is also a form of appropriation of the external world – we make a claim about the external world as an expansion of our own personality (cf. Hegel [1821] 1986: §44ff.). By buying something, we are saying: "This is who I am".

We show who we are by, for instance, engaging in what Veblen described as "conspicuous consumption" in *The Theory of the Leisure Class* (1899). The conspicuous consumer "wastes" his or her money in order to display social status. One of Veblen's examples is the use of silver cutlery at meals, when cutlery made of steel would in fact be more functional. An even clearer example would be the importance of brands in consumption, but branding had not yet made much of an impact on the consumer market when Veblen wrote his book. A more important change from Veblen's days is that he wrote about an economic elite because they were the only ones who really could afford to engage in such consumer activities, whereas today consumerism involves virtually everyone except for the very poorest. The affluent society is a society in which "good citizens" frenetically attempt to show who they are by shopping. Those who do not have the means to fully partici-pate in the feast of consumption will be shut out from a significant part of contemporary culture. If consumption is crucial for self-realization in our society, and self-realization is the most fundamental activity for the late modern individual, it is hard to avoid the conclusion that the poor fail miserably to live up to the cultural norms of our day.

What about the rest, those who can fully take part in consumption? Will they manage to become who they are by means of consumption? In *The Philosophy of Money* (1900), Georg Simmel describes consumption as a privileged field for the formation of identity, because the human self is formed by interaction with objects. Such formation requires a symbolic integration of the object in the subject's self-conception. Simmel argues that this integration is far more difficult when one purchases an object than when one have made it oneself. There is greater symbolic distance between the object and the consumer. He further points out that the vast quantity of purchasable objects in the modern world will tend to overwhelm the consumer, which makes this task of integration even harder. The typical consumer will therefore often fail to achieve such integration of the objects in his or her life plan, and as a consequence objects will tend to control the consumer, rather than the other way round.

Consumption is in fact not a very robust tool for the formation of identity, but it might have other redeeming features. I do not deny that shopping in itself can be a highly entertaining activity, but as we accumulate more and more possessions, we have less and less time to spend on each of them, and they will therefore also be of less significance. Actually, it can be misleading to describe the consumer society in terms of "accumulation". The original meaning of "consumption" is to destroy or devour. Current patterns of consumption are approaching this meaning of the word, as it is no longer as much about accumulation as about the *substitution* of goods: the endless replacement of objects with new objects.

Smith wrote surprisingly little about consumption, given the fact that he argued that it was "the sole end and purpose of all production", but he was very clear-sighted on one point:

The rich man consumes no more food than his poor neigh-
bour. In quality it may be very different, and to select and
prepare it may require more labour and art; but in quantity
it is very nearly the same. But compare the spacious palace
and great wardrobe of the one, with the hovel and the few
rags of the other, and you will be sensible that the difference
between their cloathing, lodging, and household furniture, is
almost as great in quantity as it is in quality. The desire of food
is limited in every man by the narrow capacity of the human
stomach; but the desire of the conveniencies and ornaments
of building, dress, equipage, and household furniture, seems
to have no limit or certain boundary. Those, therefore, who
have the command of more food than they themselves can
consume, are always willing to exchange the surplus, or, what
is the same thing, the price of it, for gratifications of this other
kind. What is over and above satisfying the limited desire, is
given for the amusement of those desires which cannot be
satisfied, but seem to be altogether endless.

([1776] 1981: 180–81)

He points out something that has been a crucial point in recent
theories of consumption by sociologists such as Jean Baudrillard
and Zygmunt Bauman: when consumption is ruled by *needs* it will
be limited, but when it is ruled by *desires* it is endless. The finishing
line never comes any closer. We will never be satisfied. In the words
of the British pop group The The, "I'm just another Western guy/
With desires that I can't satisfy" ("Slow Train to Dawn", Johnson
1986).

Since a life consisting only of consumption would fail to satisfy
us, there still seems to be an important role for work to play as an
essential source of meaning and identity. There is some truth to the
claim that the society of producers has been replaced by the society
of consumers, but only some. In fact, I believe that the essential

change has not been so much that consumption has replaced work as a source of identity, but rather that it has transformed our relation to work.

The norms that govern the domain of consumption are shaping our expectations of work, even to the point of replacing the traditional work ethic. It is here, I believe, that we find the main explanation for the extremely rapid and radical change in the attitude towards work in recent years. In *The Gay Science*, Nietzsche writes:

> Seeking work for the sake of wages – in this nearly all people in civilised countries are alike; to all of them, work is just a means and not itself the end, which is why they are unrefined in their choice of work, provided it yields an ample reward. Now there are rare individuals who would rather perish than work without taking *pleasure* in their work: they are choosy, hard to please, and have no use for ample rewards if the work is not itself the reward of rewards.   ([1882] 2001: §42)

This attitude to work, which Nietzsche identifies with the few, noble souls, is in fact becoming increasingly common. People who join the workforce today have expectations that differ from those of previous generations. We demand meaningful jobs in which we are self-governing and that form and confirm our identities. Work and consumption are just different arenas for what is essentially the same basic quest for self-realization. We are "shopping" for new jobs, taking them up and leaving them at a frequently higher pace. One could say that we "consume" jobs. And just as we leave consumer objects behind when they fail to satisfy us, we do the same with our jobs. When we buy a new pair of shoes or a television we know that we will replace them in the not too distant future. The same principle applies to jobs. When we start a new job, we know that we will leave it, move on to another job, in the not too distant future.

Conventional wisdom when my father started his career was: be loyal to the company and the company will be loyal to you. Hardly anyone believes that these days. Work is not like a marriage anymore. (Although given current divorce rates, one could argue that it is exactly like a marriage: it probably will not last for very long.) Bauman writes that "the prospect of constructing a life-long identity on the foundation of work is, for the great majority of people (except, for the time being at least, the practitioners of a few highly skilled and highly privileged professions), dead and buried" (2004: 27). Bauman seems to presuppose that the end of the concept of lifelong employment is something that is imposed on people against their will. There is more than a hint of nostalgia for the "good old days". He seems to overlook the possibility that, in the current labour market, lifelong employment is not necessarily what people want. The average company will experience half of its employees leaving it for another company within five years, and companies are struggling more and more to keep their employees. Nobody forces all these people to move on to new companies. They usually choose to do so because they believe that they will find that more rewarding in some way.

We tend to follow the logic of Pickles the guide dog in the animation-series *Creature Comforts*:

> If you work every day and you're doing something you don't enjoy then life must be so miserable, you know, and if you're doing something you don't enjoy, I don't know why you don't just give it up and do something you do enjoy because, you know, you may as well enjoy life because you don't live for very long so you may as well enjoy what you're doing when you are working and I really enjoy what I do and if I ever did something that I didn't enjoy then I'd give it up immediately and do something that I really did enjoy because I like to enjoy life, you know.   (Aardman Animations & Parks 2003)

It seems to be a valid point: we should enjoy our work, as it takes up so much of our limited time on earth. But then the question is: couldn't another job be even more enjoyable and more fulfilling than the current one? The problem is that the next job will also turn out to be disappointing, so we move on to yet another job, which becomes another disappointment.

I am certainly painting a bleak picture here. Is that picture accurate? I believe that there is some truth to it, but only some. Studies of job satisfaction make it clear that people do not experience their jobs as constant sources of disappointment. Job satisfaction is consistently high in the Western world, and it has been so for decades. Eighty to ninety per cent of employees say that they are either completely or mostly happy with their jobs. There has been a slight change among the youngest and oldest workers, as younger workers are slightly more satisfied than they used to be and older workers are slightly less satisfied, but the overall numbers are the same as before. Full-time and part-time workers are equally satisfied. So people are generally happy with their jobs, and yet staff turnover is rising every year. So they are not so happy that they plan to stay in a job for very long, at least not compared to the average worker only a couple of decades ago. We are constantly searching for something better, more fulfilling or prestigious – or we simply want a change.

We still believe that work is an importance source of meaning and identity. We still need work, for existential reasons, in the midst of our abundance. Consumption simply does not manage to fill this existential need. What should we do if work is coming to an end, as some have argued?

8. The end of work?

I have not lived in my hometown, Moss, for almost twenty years, but I visit my family there frequently. It has undergone substantial change in a few decades. One could hardly fail to notice the dwindling number of workers leaving the factory gates at the end of the day. It became increasingly clear that no more tankers would leave the shipyard, and then the glass factory and the concrete factory were shut down. The paper mill, which is the source of the town's distinctive smell, is still there, but apart from that there is little industry left in what used to be an industrial town. This probably sounds like the beginning of a sad story of mass unemployment in a small industrial town without industry. In fact, there is virtually no unemployment in Moss, and it has been that way for most of the time since the factories were shut down. New jobs were created, and they more than replaced the old ones. These days Moss looks more or less like one big shopping mall, and even if I can be nostalgic about the old industry – as the factories always had a certain aesthetic appeal to me – the transition from the industrial to the post-industrial society seems to have been fairly painless.

Moss hosts a festival for contemporary art, and some years ago a well-meaning artist who had heard that the festival was held in an industrial town in decline wanted to make an installation for the poor souls who had no jobs and so had nothing to do during the day. The installation was called *Cinema for the Unemployed*, and consisted of several Hollywood disaster movies being shown in a cinema, jokingly indicating that the unemployed could have been far worse off. The artist asked me to write something for the catalogue that would accompany the installation. I wrote a short piece predicting that virtually nobody would turn up to watch the movies; my prediction turned out to be accurate. During the three weeks the installation was shown, only a handful of people showed up. Where were the rest? They were at work, since there were hardly any unemployed people in the town. There is nothing atypical about Moss in this regard. The trend throughout the Western world has been that even though jobs are lost to outsourcing and labour-saving technologies, more new jobs are created than the ones that are lost.

At the time of writing, unemployment figures in OECD countries are fairly low. The average unemployment rate for these countries is 5.5 per cent (OECD 2008: 1). There are not many indications that the figures will rise significantly any time soon, even though they will fluctuate somewhat over time. Some might argue that even our current unemployment figures are too high, but historically speaking they are quite low. Any nostalgia about the "good" old days could be countered by remembering that unemployment in London in 1850 was, by some estimates, as high as 40 per cent.

If past and present development are reliable guides to the future, there is little reason to worry. However, it is conceivable that the past and present are in fact not reliable guides, because we are at the very beginning of a transformation of the entire field of labour. This is Jeremy Rifkin's argument. He offers a depressing vision of the future of work, summarized in the title of his book, *The End of Work* (1995). According to Rifkin, computers will eliminate jobs on a large scale. This is essentially a restatement of Marx's claim that machines would replace human labour as labour itself was increasingly mechanized. Modern technology transforms the operations workers perform into increasingly mechanical operations, thereby setting the stage for a replacement of the worker with a machine. Marx wrote:

Thus we can see directly how a particular form of labour is transferred from the worker to capital in the form of the machine and his own labour power is devalued as a result of this transposition. Hence we have the struggle of the worker against machinery.   (quoted in Braverman 1974: 278)

The capitalist wants this because machines would be more cost-efficient than workers and give capitalists complete control of production. And Henry Ford seemed to confirm Marx's prediction when he said in an interview published in the *Chicago Tribune* newspaper, "At least I don't have to deal with the robot's union". Ultimately the development of technology would lead to the elimination of the worker. Marx saw an irony here: the capitalist would dig his own grave because the elimination of the worker would also be the elimination of the consumer because there would be virtually no people left with money to purchase the product, and in turn that would be the end of capitalism itself. Of course, Marx's prediction missed its mark completely: exactly the opposite has happened. My guess is that Rifkin's prediction will fare no better.

Technology appears to be Janus-faced, as it is both a liberator and a threat. It liberates us from having to do work that instead can be done by machinery, but that also means that workers are rendered superfluous. In *The Soul of Man under Socialism*, Oscar Wilde argued that "there is something tragic in the fact that as soon as man had invented a machine to do his work he began to starve" ([1891] 2001: 140). Wilde lamented that as soon as machines were installed, people became unemployed. On the other hand, he also argued that the sort of work that machines can do is exactly the kind of work that man should not have to do:

All unintellectual labour, all monotonous, dull labour, all labour that deals with dreadful things, and involves unpleasant conditions, must be done by machinery. Machinery must work for us in coal mines, and do all sanitary services, and be the stoker of steamers, and clean the streets, and run messages on wet days, and do anything that is tedious or distressing.

(Ibid.)

Wilde's solution to this is socialism: the machines should be owned by the community, and the entire community – not only particular factory owners – should benefit from them. Would such a world be a happy one?

You can find a fictional presentation of such a world in Kurt Vonnegut's first novel, *Player Piano* (1952), which takes place in a future society in which computers and automation takes care of virtually all production. Very few people have to work and everyone is provided for, but it is an unhappy society because people have not managed to find their way about in a world without work. Only an elite of managers and engineers has work and a sense of purpose in life. The novel's protagonist, Paul Proteus, is an engineer who joins a revolutionary group called the Ghost Shirt Society. They destroy a lot of machinery, but the novel ends in the realization that they cannot overthrow the workless society.

The Ghost Shirt Society in Vonnegut's novel is a neo-Luddite group. The original Luddites existed for only a few years, from 1811 to 1816; they were groups of men who protested against the changes being brought about by the Industiral Revolution by destroying machinery, especially in the textile industry. Luddites took their name from a man called Ned Ludd, who in 1779 broke into a house in Leicestershire and destroyed two stocking frames. After this episode, people started attributing the sabotage of any piece of machinery, especially stocking frames, to Ludd. There has hardly been a single technological innovation that has not been fiercely attacked by later generations of Luddites, even though the attacks have usually been verbal rather than physical.

The Luddite fallacy, an economic fallacy named after the nineteenth-century protestors, is the belief that labour-saving technologies lead to increased unemployment because the demand for labour is reduced. The idea seems reasonable enough, but it is a fallacy because labour-saving technologies increase workers' productivity, which lowers the cost of goods, which in turn increases demand. With an increase in the demand for the goods, there will not necessarily be a decrease in the demand for labour. If the Luddites had been right in thinking that labour-saving technologies lead to unemployment, hardly any of us would have had a job today, given the extreme technological development there has been over the past two centuries. One could be tempted to argue that the explanation for why automation has not led to more unemployment is that working hours have fallen dramatically, but the increase in productivity has been many times higher than the decrease in working hours. Average working hours today are half of those in 1850, but produce twenty-five times more value.

Technology-driven mass unemployment has so far never occurred. The truth is simply that the jobs lost to technology have been more than replaced by the creation of new jobs. This also holds for the computer age. If we look at the UK between 1970 and 2000, 3.5 million industrial jobs were lost, but in the same period total employment increased by 6.4 million, which means that 10 million new jobs were created in this period. The general development has been the same in most Western countries. The trend since Rifkin's book was published in 1995 does not support his claims. In the USA alone 20 million new jobs have been created in this period.

New technology destroys and creates jobs, and so far the net effect has been that it has created far more jobs than it has destroyed. Will this continue? We have no guarantee that it will. It is doubtful that we can make any sensible assessment of future labour markets, for the simple reason that we do not today know what the innovations of tomorrow will be. It is notoriously difficult to predict what jobs will be in high demand only a few years from now. The labour market can change quickly. In the 1980s how many people would have predicted that website designers would soon be in high demand? Hardly any, but in the 1990s it seemed as if every other person one ran into was a website designer. When the dotcom-bubble burst, many of them were out of work. Suddenly all the waiters at cafés and restaurants who claimed to "really" be actors were joined by waiters who said that they were "really" website designers. Many now seem to have moved on to become baristas, at least in my neighbourhood, where the cafés are so numerous that they are virtually wall-to-wall. Ten years ago, the market for website designers was booming and baristas were not in high demand. It is equally hard to predict what sorts of jobs will be in demand ten years from now.

Speculations about the end of work have tended to focus on the introduction of new technologies. However, in the retail sector the introduction of self-service stores has had a far greater impact than any technological innovations. There has also been a large increase in products that the consumer must assemble at home, such as the flat-pack furniture from IKEA. I wonder how many IKEA-bookshelves I have assembled over the past 15–20 years, and how many four-letter words I have shouted on these occasions, since I definitely have not inherited my father's talents as a handyman. To some extent, then, the consumer becomes producer, so it adds to the blurring of the line between them. One would think that this would lead to unemployment, as factories and stores need fewer staff because the customers do so much work themselves. On the contrary, it has increased demand – since flat-pack furniture is relatively inexpensive – and therefore also employment.

Some might say that employment may have increased, but it has done so elsewhere, as production has been outsourced. Actually, outsourcing often leads to an *increase* in the number of staff at home.

This has been documented especially clearly in the IT sector, where a study by economists Nariman Behravesh and Lawrence Klein, the latter a Nobel Laureate, concluded that outsourcing *increased* employment in the US and also lead to a rise in workers' real wages (Behravesh 2005). By outsourcing some services, the companies get resources to expand and hire more staff. For instance, when Delta Airlines outsourced 1000 call-centre jobs to India in 2003, they saved $25 million, which they used to hire 1200 salesmen in the US.

So far, all warnings about the end of work have failed to come true. Instead, the past decades have been years of remarkable growth, of constant creation of new jobs, even though there are significant differences between nations. We cannot rule out the possibility that work as we know it will come to an end at some point, but we can be fairly confident that it will not happen any time soon.

In *The Human Condition*, Hannah Arendt argues that the modern world has been one that has glorified labour to such an extent that we have lost sight of what human life could or should be without it: "It is a society of laborers which is about to be liberated from the fetters of labor, and this society does no longer know of those other higher and more meaningful activities for the sake of which this freedom would deserve to be won" (1958: 5). One can hardly disagree with her claim that modern culture has had work at the very centre of its ideology, but I seriously disagree with her claim that we are about to be "liberated" from work. Arendt's problem is that she is so committed to her own notion of work that she fails to see that work does not disappear; it is transformed. The "end of work" is not in our foreseeable future. Work will continue its transformations, and much of what passes for work today – and probably even more so in the world of tomorrow – will probably look a lot like what earlier generations would have called leisure. However, it will still be work if we regard it as work.

9. Life and work

One thing I have in common with the famous philosopher of science Paul Feyerabend is that as children we both gave the same answer to the question of what we wanted to become when we grew up: "I want to retire". It seemed patently obvious that retired people were living the good life, sitting on benches and doing very little indeed, just enjoying themselves, whereas working people were in such a hurry and did not seem nearly as privileged. It was a great disappointment to be told that I actually had to work for many years before I could retire. Towards the end of his autobiography *Killing Time*, Feyerabend writes: "And so, at long last, my childish wish became reality: I was a retired person" (1995: 168). Yet, there is a sense of regret, as he laments not having much direction in life any more and wonders about what to do with his newfound freedom. I am thirty years away from the age when I am supposed to retire, and that is such a long time that I have no clear idea about what retired life would be like. There are of course days when I return to the dream of not having to work another day in my entire life, but I guess that I would quickly become bored.

Jeremy Bentham wrote: "In so far as *labour* is taken in its proper sense, *love of labour* is a contradiction in terms" (1983: 104). Of course we can love labour, but that is also a potential problem. We can come to love our job so much that we overlook things that, at the end of the day, are far more important. I am speaking from experience. For a couple of years, I was probably more in love with my work than in anything else – at least it seems so in retrospect, when I look at what my priorities were – but I did not notice it while it happened. It started when I won a generous four-year scholarship to write a dissertation on Kant's theory of interpretation. I really worked hard on that project: so hard that I finished it several months before the money ran out. Great, I thought, now I can enjoy doing absolutely nothing for months. The problem was that "doing nothing" quickly became excruciatingly boring. I was so bored that I had to write a book on boredom just to overcome the overwhelming sense of emptiness. To my great surprise, the book did well, and that made me so busy with interviews and lectures that I did not have time to be bored: that is, until I got used to all the interviews and the travelling to various places for lectures, and got increasingly bored with that. I started longing to just sit at my desk at home and write another book or two. I continued to work hard, and in five years I wrote and published seven books, took a job as an associate professor at a university, became the editor of the *Norwegian Journal of Philosophy*, gave lectures outside the university every week, was a columnist for a national newspaper, co-hosted a talk show on national television, gave a couple of interviews every week and so on.

That sounds like a description of a genuine workaholic. The problem was that even though all those activities for the most part were sources of satisfaction, work – like so many other phenomena – is a case of diminishing returns. Working so much meant that I had too little time for my family and friends, and at the end of the day they matter a whole lot more to me than any job has ever done. In my years as a workaholic I still believed that I put my family and friends above my work, but the real priorities in my everyday life were clear evidence of the opposite. In a moment of clarity – and I must admit that in my life those are few and far apart – I realised that I had to cut down significantly on my workload. I did not stop working, but I settled for a considerably shorter working week, slightly above average working hours. I am still on that level, which suits me fine. The Protestant work ethic is still lodged in my spine, however, and were I to work significantly less than that I would probably be overcome by strong feelings of guilt. Work is still important to me, but I am no longer willing to let it overshadow all other things in life.

This makes me a less than ideal worker in today's labour market. The ideal, flexible worker is one with "zero drag". It is a rather new expression, and the earliest citation I have found is from 1999:

> Everything is faster. Zero drag is optimal. For a while, new applicants would jokingly be asked about their "drag coefficient." Since the office is a full hour's commute from San Francisco, an apartment in the city was a full unit of drag. A spouse? Drag coefficient of one. Kids? A half point per."
>
> (Bronson 1999)

The "zero drag" employee is young, unmarried and childless, has no responsibilities towards aging parents and can put in long hours whenever the company needs it. The "zero drag" employee is one who can put the needs of the company at the very top of his or her list of priorities. The company in turn wants to facilitate this, and more and more companies provide their employees with services that would usually occupy their leisure time, such as keep fit studios, takeaway meals and cleaning. In this way the employee is supposed to perceive of the company as his or her primary community. It should be noted that such services are provided to a far greater extent to employees in middle and top management than to those further down the corporate ladder. There is little reason to believe that companies do this out of the goodness of their hearts; the idea is that providing such services will improve productivity because the employee can stay another hour or two in the office. The "caring company" cares because it is profitable. Doing something because it is profitable is a perfectly legitimate motivation, but one should be honest about what the real motivation is. One might even say that the zero-drag employee should ideally not even have any friends outside the office, as that might also take valuable time away from the company. It would presumably be much better if one's friends were identical with the people one works with. However, the people one works with are not usually one's closest friends. As Tim in *The Office* puts it:

> The people you work with are people you were just thrown together with. I mean, you don't know them, it wasn't your choice. And yet you spend more time with them than you do your friends or your family. But probably all you have in common is the fact that you walk around on the same bit of carpet for eight hours a day.   (Gervais & Merchant 2003)

But in the case of the genuine zero-drag worker, it would be fifteen hours a day.

The elimination of the distinctions between job and hobby, work and leisure, can make work into the central axis around which everything in life revolves. Work becomes a second home or even the place where we feel most at home. The job can seem to bring us most of the meaning we need in life. If we actually believe that we have found such a job, we are probably well on the way to losing sight of the truly important things in life. There is always a danger when a particular source of meaning comes to dominate all the others, and from recognizing the value of work in establishing a sense of self-worth and purpose in life it is a long step to going to the extreme where work becomes the very essence of life. We should not believe Thomas Carlyle: "Blessed is he who has found his work; let him ask no other blessedness. He has a work, a life-purpose; he has found it, and will follow it!" ([1843] 1965: 197). I would rather say that cursed is he who believes that there is nothing more to life than work.

If we are aiming for happiness in life – and we are if Aristotle was right in arguing that happiness is the only thing we aim for as an end in itself – then work will probably play an important role in our quest for happiness. We should be aware, then, that such aspects of work as higher wages and promotions usually have very little impact on our overall satisfaction. It appears that the internal goods of work are far more important than the external ones. But we can also get hooked on the internal goods of work, and then we might be in big trouble, simply because work comes across as so satisfying. Even in today's flexible and more disjointed work life, work is in some ways a more stable and trustworthy part of our life than many other things. For instance, our statistical chances of getting divorced are significantly higher than our chances of getting fired. Our job can be far less demanding than our spouse, at least Samuel Pepys thought so, and wrote the following in his diary entry for 7 November 1668: "Up, and at the office all morning; and so to it again after dinner and there busy late, choosing to employ myself rather than go home to trouble with my wife" (quoted in Thomas 1999: 159). Pepys was a notorious workaholic.

The term "workaholic" was coined by Rev. Wayne E. Oates in 1968. Oates was a very hard-working writer and Baptist minister, who had little time for his family. One day his five-year-old son asked for an appointment to see him. Oates got the message, and realized that there was something wrong with the way he had chosen to live. In 1971 he published the book *Confessions of a Workaholic*, which introduced the word to a broader public. Oates hardly set a good example for others: he ended up writing fifty-seven books before he died in 1999.

For the workaholic work appears to be an end in itself rather than a means to an end. Everything revolves around the job for the workaholic. He is an addict. What separates the addict from a "normal" person? That depends on the nature of the addiction, but a general feature of all addictions is that the thing one is addicted to – be it a drug, sex or work – becomes the dominant source of meaning in life. Everything else revolves around this dominant source of meaning. In the film *Trainspotting* (1996), the main character points out that whereas life is full of various problems for the ordinary person, the drug addict has managed to reduce everything to a single – if large – problem. The workaholic is not all that different from the drug addict in that respect.

There is also much more to happiness than work. A famous literary example of someone who overlooked this is the main character in Leo Tolstoy's novella *The Death of Ivan Ilyich* (1886). Ivan becomes increasingly obsessed with his official duties at work. When he gets married, his main concern is that the marriage might disrupt his work life. What makes this such a sad story is that before he dies Ivan recognizes that he has wasted his life: that his total absorption in work has made him miss out on so many things, most importantly close relations with other people.

Human life is messy, rich and multifaceted. No other animal displays such a great range of possibilities. Even if we have found what appears to be the perfect job, the kind of work we appear to be made for, the job will fail to engage us as a whole human being. It is fairly obvious: we need something more in life than just work. A job is not a life.

Most people are probably in a situation where their job fails to satisfy them completely, and that can in itself make them unhappy. As Morrissey sang in The Smiths's song: "I was looking for a job, and then I found a job/And heaven knows I'm miserable now" (Morrissey & Marr 1984). We often have totally unrealistic expectations of what a job might be, as we currently have of most other things in life. We no longer search for spiritual salvation, but for complete happiness. But happiness is no longer something we all have the right to *search* for, but has rather become something we are all *entitled* to. Whoever fails to realize complete happiness is basically a loser. The French philosopher Pascal Bruckner has pointed out that we probably live in the first society where people are unhappy simply because they fail to realize complete happiness (2000: 76). The failure to achieve a state of complete happiness, which is a completely unrealistic ideal, in itself makes us miserable. So if we are unhappy with our lives, we should perhaps take a minute to consider the possibility that the problem is not necessarily the job in itself, but rather our expectations of it.

We will all find our job boring from time to time. The question is whether or not we can accept and live with this boredom. Joseph Brodsky points out that "you'll be bored with your work, your friends, your spouses, your lovers, the view from your window, the furniture or wallpaper in your room, your thoughts, yourselves" (1996: 109). To escape this boredom, we change job, friends, partner, wallpaper and flat and start anew. Life becomes a series of beginnings. Rather than Nietzsche's notion of the eternal recurrence of the same, our lives become structured by what Walter Benjamin described as the essence of fashion: the eternal recurrence of the *new* (1991: 677). However, this is hardly an ideal for living. As Brodsky writes:

> Basically, there is nothing wrong with turning life into the constant quest for alternatives, into leapfrogging jobs, spouses, and surroundings, provided that you can afford the alimony and jumbled memories. This predicament, after all, has been sufficiently glamorized onscreen and in Romantic poetry. The rub, however, is that before long this quest turns into a full-time occupation, with your need for an alternative coming to match a drug addict's daily fix.   (1996: 109)

If that is our approach, we are definitely letting boredom run our entire life, since we spend all our time trying to escape boredom. And all things will disappoint us if we set our expectations too high. Disappointment presupposes expectations, and if we have very high expectations, the likelihood of disappointment is all the greater. If we expect work to provide us with the ultimate meaning in life, we will be disappointed. The same holds for love, friendship, art and all other things. There is no ultimate meaning. Nothing is sufficient in itself.

On the other hand, the solution to this problem is hardly to become a fully fledged cynic. The original Cynics were group of philosophers in ancient Greece who recognized that life is difficult and believed that they had found the perfect way to deal with this. Their philosophy can be summarized as: nothing really matters. There is a lot more to be said about the Cynics, but this is really what it all comes down to. They were totally wrong, of course. All sorts of things matter.

Since work has become much more unstable than it used to be – we certainly do not have a job for life any more – it might seem wise to rely less on it for our sense of ourself. However, such an attitude might lead to an indifference towards work, and then it certainly will not contribute much to our life, except as a source of income. I believe that we should rather commit ourselves to work, as such commitment is a precondition of finding genuine meaning in it, but on the other hand, work should only be regarded as one source of meaning among others. Woody Allen said "I don't want to achieve immortality through my work … I want to achieve it through not dying". Since immortality is not an option, we should probably settle for something slightly less ambitious, such as a fairly balanced life.

As I wrote in the introduction to this book, I have not defended a specific "thesis" about work or presented the reader with instructions as to how they should relate to work. It is nevertheless clear that a certain picture of work has emerged, one in which we do not work particularly hard compared to people earlier in history, where most of us are extremely well off in terms of material wealth, and where our expectations of work have never been higher. I also quoted Wittgenstein, who defined philosophy as a: "work on oneself. On one's own conception. On the way one sees things. (And what one expects of them.)" (1998: 12). My impression is that we generally expect too much from work these days, more specifically that it should be able to bring us so much of the meaning we need in our lives. Those expectations will probably not be met, and we become nomads at work, going from one job to another, never finding what we are looking for. If our expectations are met, we are probably in even deeper trouble, as we then will be in danger of ignoring all those things that matter more than our job. Our relation to work would then appear to be a perfect illustration of Wilde's claim in *Lady Windermere's Fan*: "In this world there are only two tragedies. One is not getting what one wants, and the other is getting it. The last is much the worst; the last is a real tragedy!" ([1892] 1997: 519). Few of us, however, would describe our work life simply as a tragedy: work is a curse for some people, a blessing for others and a little bit of both for most of us. Work has changed immensely in a very short time, and we have to figure out for ourselves what relevance it might have in our lives.

Further reading

A large number of short texts and quotations about work can be found in Keith Thomas's edited collection *The Oxford Book of Work* (1999). A selection of longer texts on work from a great variety of sources (fiction, philosophy, theology, social sciences and so on) is available in Gilbert C. Meilaender's edited collection *Working* (2000). Several contemporary philosophical texts on work are compiled in Kory Schaff's edited collection *Philosophy and the Problems of Work* (2001). All three books are highly recommended for readers who want to study the topic further. For an overview of recent sociological research on work, see Keith Grint's edited collection *Work and Society* (2001). His *The Sociology of Work* (2005) is also recommended.

A proper understanding of what work is today presupposes an understanding of the historical development of work, and Richard Donkin does an excellent job of presenting this in *Blood, Sweat & Tears* (2001). Among the best philosophical essays on work in recent years is Russell Muirhead's *Just Work* (2004), which investigates the idea of a "fit" between who we are as persons and our work life from the ancient Greeks to the present day. Al Gini's *My Job, My Self* (2001) combines the best of philosophical and sociological theory, and provides the reader with a wealth of insight into the contemporary role of work in our lives. His book presents a slightly bleaker picture of work than I have done in this essay, so it should come as no surprise that he also wrote a sequel about *not* working, *The Importance of Being Lazy* (2003), which is also highly recommended. When studying laziness, you should also check out Tom Hodgkinson's *How to be Idle* (2005). One of the most interesting studies of work–life balance is Arlie Russell Hochschild's *The Time Bind* (1997). Most people would agree that work has been transformed significantly in the past decades, but there is also a tendency in much literature to exaggerate the extent of these changes. For an excellent antidote to such exaggerations, see Harriet Bradley *et al*.'s *Myths at Work* (2000).

For a discussion of how consumerism has shaped our relation to work, see Paul du Gay's *Consumption and Identity at Work* (1996). This is also a central point in Zygmunt Bauman's *Work, Consumerism and the New Poor* (2007), but his most central concern is the plight of the poor in a society of consumers. A far more optimistic picture of the current state of our societies is presented by Brink Lindsay in *The Age of Abundance* (2007), which points out that we – and that includes the poor – have never been better off in terms of material wealth at any time in human history. Many would argue that Lindsay paints a far too rosy picture of modern capitalism, and among them we find Richard Sennett, who has argued in books such as *The Corrosion of Character* (1998) and *The Culture of the New Capitalism* (2006) that the current variety of capitalism has grave consequences for our very identities: that it in fact undermines our attempt at forming a personal identity. We can always learn much from Sennett's books, whether we agree with him or not.

References

Aardman Animations (Producer), Nick Parks (Director) 2003. *Creature Comforts: The Complete Series 1, Episode 3: Working Animals* [DVD]. Momentum Pictures.

Arendt, H. 1958. *The Human Condition*. Chicago, IL: University of Chicago Press.

Aristotle 1985a. *Politics*, B. Jowett (trans.). In *The Complete Works of Aristotle*, vol. 2. Princeton, NJ: Princeton University Press.

Aristotle 1985b. *Nicomachean Ethics*, W. D. Ross (trans.). In *The Complete Works of Aristotle*, vol. 2. Princeton, NJ: Princeton University Press.

Bauman, Z. 2004. *Work, Consumerism and the New Poor*, 2nd edn. Buckingham: Open University Press.

Behravesh, N. 2005. *The Impact of Offshore Software and IT Services Outsourcing on the US Economy and the IT Industry*. Boston, MA: Global Insight.

Benedict 1998. *The Rule of Saint Benedict*, T. Fry (trans.). New York: Vintage.

Benjamin, W. 1991. *Zentralpark, Gesammelte Schiften Band I*. Frankfurt: Suhrkamp.

Bentham, J. [1787] 1995. *Panopticon*. In *The Panopticon Writings*, M. Bozovic (ed.). London: Verso.

Bentham, J. 1983. *Deontology. Together with a Table of the Springs of Action and Article on Utilitarianism*. Oxford: Clarendon Press.

Bradley, H., M. Erickson, C. Stephenson & S. Williams 2000. *Myths at Work*. Cambridge: Polity.

Braverman, H. 1974. *Labor and Monopoly Capital: The Degradation of Work in the Twentieth Century*. New York: Monthly Review Press.

Brodsky, J. 1996. *On Grief and Reason: Essays*. London: Hamish Hamilton.

Bronson, P. 1999. "Instant Company". *New York Times* (11 July): 44–7.

Bruckner, P. 2000. *Verdammt zum Glück. Der Fluch der Moderne*. Berlin: Aufbau Verlag.

Camus, A. [1942] 1991. *The Myth of Sisyphus and Other Essays*, J. O'Brien (trans.). New York: Vintage.

Carlyle, T. [1843] 1965. *Past and Present*. Boston, MA: Houghton Mifflin.

Chapman G., M. Palin, J. Cleese *et al.* 2001. *The Monty Python's Life of Brian (of Nazareth): Screenplay*. London: Methuen

Chesterton, G. K. 1970. *A Selection from His Non-Fictional Prose*. London: Faber.

Csíkszentmihályi, M. 1990. *Flow: The Psychology of Optimal Experience*. New York: Harper & Row.

Donkin, R. 2001. *Blood, Sweat & Tears: The Evolution of Work*. New York: Texere.

Dostoyevsky, F. [1862] 1986. *The House of the Dead*, D. McDuff (trans.). Harmondsworth: Penguin.

du Gay, P. 1996. *Consumption and Identity at Work*. London: Sage.

Ehrenreich, B. 2001. *Nickel and Dimed*. New York: Metropolitan Books.

Ferris. J. 2007. *Then We Came to the End*. London: Viking.

Feyerabend, P. 1995. *Killing Time*. Chicago, IL: University of Chicago Press.

Florida, R. 2002. *The Rise of the Creative Class: And How It's Transforming Work, Leisure, Community and Everyday Life*. New York: Basic Books.

Ford, H. & S. Crowther [1922] 2003. *My Life and Work*. Whitefish, MT: Kessinger.

Franklin, B. 1987. *Writings*. New York: Library of America.

Galbraith, J. K. 1958. *The Affluent Society*. New York: Mariner Books.

Gersemann, O. 2005. *Cowboy Capitalism: European Myths about the American Reality*, 2nd edn. Washington, DC: Cato Institute.

Gervais, R. & S. Merchant 2003. *The Office: The Scripts*. London: BBC Books.

Gini, A. 2001. *My Job, My Self: Work and the Creation of the Modern Individual*. London: Routledge.

Gini, A. 2003. *The Importance of Being Lazy: In Praise of Play, Leisure and Vacations*. London: Routledge.

Grint, K. (ed.) 2001. *Work and Society: A Reader*. Cambridge: Polity.

Grint, K. 2005. *The Sociology of Work*, 3rd edn. Cambridge: Polity.

Hegel, G. W. F. [1821] 1986. *Grundlinien der Philosophie des Rechts (Werke 7)*. Frankfurt: Suhrkamp.

Herodotus 1996. *Histories*, G. Rawlinson (trans.). Ware: Wordsworth Classics.

Hesiod 1999. *Works and Days*. In *Theogony, Works and Days*, M. L. West (trans.). Oxford: Oxford University Press.

Hobbes. T. [1657] 1991. *De Homine*. In *Man and Citizen: De Homine and De Cive*, C. T. Wood et al. (trans.). Indianapolis, IN: Hackett.

Hochschild, A. R. 2000. *The Time Bind: When Work Becomes Home and Home Becomes Work*, 2nd edn. New York: Henry Holt.

Hodgkinson, T. 2005. *How to be Idle*. Harmondsworth: Penguin.

Hughes, T. P. 2004. *American Genesis: A Century of Invention and Technological Enthusiasm 1870–1970*, 2nd edn. Chicago, IL: University of Chicago Press.

Huxley, A. 1932. *Brave New World*. London: Chatto & Windus.

James, W. 1915. *The Will to Believe and Other Essays in Popular Philosophy*. New York: Longman, Green.

Jensen, J. B. 2001. "Fremtidens arbejdsbegreb". Copenhagen: Copenhagen Institute for Futures Studies.

Johnson, M. 1986. "Slow Train to Dawn" [The The]. On *Infected* [CD]. © Complete Music Ltd/CBS Inc./Epic Inc.

Johnson, S. [1758] 2003. *The Idler*. In his *Selected Essays*. Harmondsworth: Penguin.

Kant, I. [1785] 1998. *Groundwork of the Metaphysics of Morals*, M. Gregor (trans.). Cambridge: Cambridge University Press.

Kant, I. [1798] 1902–. *Anthropologie in pragmatischer Hinsicht*. In *Kants gesammelte Schriften*, vol. VII. Berlin: de Gruyter.

Kant, I. [1803] 1902–. *Pädagogik*. In *Kants gesammelte Schriften*, vol. VII. Berlin: de Gruyter.

Kant, I. 2001. *Lectures on Ethics*, P. Heath (trans.). Cambridge: Cambridge University Press.

Keynes, J. M. [1930] 1963. *Essays in Persuasion*. New York: Norton.

Keynes, J. M. [1923] 2000. *A Tract on Monetary Reform*. Amherst, NY: Prometheus.

Kunde, J. 2000. *Corporate Religion*. London: Financial Times-Prentice Hall.

Lafargue, P. [1883] 1999. *The Right to be Lazy*, L. Bracken (trans.). New York: Fifth Season.

Lane, R. E. 2000. *The Loss of Happiness in Market Democracies*. New Haven, CT: Yale University Press.

Lenin, V. I. [1913] 1968. "A 'Scientific' System of Sweating". In his *Collected Works*, vol. 18, 4th edn. Moscow: Progress Publishers.

Lenin, V. I. [1914] 1968. "The Taylor System – Man's Enslavement by the Machine". In his *Collected Works*, vol. 20, 4th edn. Moscow: Progress Publishers.

Lenin, V. I. [2910] 2001. *Left-Wing Communism: An Infantile Disorder*. Honolulu, HI: University Press of the Pacific.

Lindsay, B. 2007. *The Age of Abundance: How Prosperity Transformed America's Politics and Culture*. New York: Collins.

Luther, M. [1520] 1915. *Prelude on the Babylonian Captivity of the Church*. In *Works of Martin Luther with Introductions and Notes*. Philadelphia: A. J. Holman.

Malachowski, D. 2005. "Wasted Time At Work Costing Companies Billions". www.salary.com/careers/layouthtmls/crel_display_nocat_Ser374_Par555.html (accessed July 2008).

Marshall, A. [1890] 1907. *Principles of Economics*. London: Macmillan.

Marx, K. [1844] 1994. "From the Paris Notebooks". In *Marx: Early Political Writings*, J. O. Malley (trans.). Cambridge, Cambridge University Press.

Marx, K. [1845] 1994. *The German Ideology*. In *Marx: Early Political Writings*, J. O. Malley (trans.). Cambridge: Cambridge University Press.

Marx, K. [1867] 1976. *Capital: Volume 1: A Critique of Political Economy*, B. Fowkes (trans.). Harmondsworth: Penguin.

Marx, K. [1875] 1996. *Critique of the Gotha Programme*. In *Marx: Later Political Writings*, T. Carver (trans.). Cambridge: Cambridge University Press.

Marx, K. [1894] 1993. *Capital: Volume 3: A Critique of Political Economy*, D. Fernbach (trans.). Harmondsworth: Penguin.

Meilaender, G. C. (ed.) 2000. *Working: Its Meaning and Its Limits*. Notre Dame, IN: University of Notre Dame Press.

Mill, J. S. [1850] 1984. *The Negro Question*. In *The Collected Works of John Stuart Mill, Volume XXI – Essays on Equality, Law, and Education*. Toronto: University of Toronto Press.

Morrissey, S. & J. Marr 1984. "Heaven Knows I'm Miserable Now" [The Smiths]. On *Hatful of Hollow* [CD]. © Warner Bros. Music Ltd.

Muirhead, R. 2004. *Just Work*. Cambridge, MA: Harvard University Press.

Nietzsche, F. [1882] 2001. *The Gay Science*, J. Nauckhoff & A. Del Caro (trans.). Cambridge: Cambridge University Press.

Nietzsche, F. [1886] 2001. *Beyond Good and Evil*, J. Norman (trans.). Cambridge: Cambridge University Press.

Nozick, R. 1974. *Anarchy, State and Utopia*. New York: Basic Books.

Oates, W. E. 1971. *Confessions of a Workaholic*. New York: World Publishing.

OECD 2008. "OECD Standardised Unemployment Rates", news release. Paris: OECD. www.oecd.org/dataoecd/10/0/40800076.pdf (accessed July 2008).

Orwell, G. [1933] 1972. *Down and Out in Paris and London*. San Diego, CA: Harvest.

Peters, T. 1982. *In Search of Excellence*. New York: Harper & Row.

Pew Research Center 2006. *Public Says American Work Life Is Worsening, But Most Workers Remain Satisfied with Their Jobs*. Washington, DC: Pew Research Center. http://pewresearch.org/assets/social/pdf/Jobs.pdf (accessed July 2008).

Plato 1989a. *Republic*, P. Shorey (trans.). In *The Collected Dialogues of Plato*. Princeton, NJ: Princeton University Press.

Plato 1989b. *Laws*, A. E. Taylor (trans.). In *The Collected Dialogues of Plato*. Princeton, NJ: Princeton University Press.

Rifkin, J. 2004. *The End of Work: The Decline of the Global Labor Force and the Dawn of the Post-Market Era*. New York: Tarcher/Penguin.

Robinson, J. & G. Godbey 1997. *Time for Life: The Surprising Ways Americans Use Their Time*. University Park, PA: Pennsylvania State University Press.

Russell, B. [1930] 1996. *The Conquest of Happiness*. New York: Liveright.

Sahlins, M. [1972] 2003. *Stone Age Economics*. London: Routledge.

Schaff, K. (ed.) 2001. *Philosophy and the Problems of Work: A Reader*. Lanham, MD: Rowman & Littlefield.

Schor, J. B. 1993. *The Overworked American: The Unexpected Decline of Leisure*. New York: Basic Books.

Seaford, R. 2004. *Money and the Early Greek Mind*. Cambridge: Cambridge University Press.

Sennett, R. 1998. *The Corrosion of Character: The Personal Consequences of Work in the New Capitalism*. New York: Norton.

Sennett, R. 2006. *The Culture of the New Capitalism*. New Haven, CT: Yale University Press.

Simmel, G. [1900] 1989. *Philosophie des Geldes, Gesamtausgabe Band 6*. Frankfurt: Suhrkamp.

Smith, A. [1776] 1981. *The Wealth of Nations*, Glasgow Edition, vol. 2. Indianapolis, IN: Liberty Fund.

Smith, A. [1759] 1982. *The Theory of Moral Sentiments*, Glasgow Edition, vol. 1. Indianapolis, IN: Liberty Fund.

Spencer, H. 1891. "A Speech: Delivered on the Occasion of a Complimentary Dinner in New York, on November 9, 1882". In his *Essays: Scientific, Political, and Speculative*, vol. 3. London: Williams & Norgate.

Taylor, F. W. [1911] 2007. *Principles of Scientific Management*. Sioux Falls, SD: Nuvision Publications.

Tennant, N. & C. Lowe 1996. "To Step Aside" [Pet Shop Boys]. On *Bilingual* [CD]. Cage Music Ltd/EMI 190 Music Ltd.

Thomas, K. (ed.) 1999. *The Oxford Book of Work*. Oxford: Oxford University Press.

Tolstoy, L. [1886] 2004. *The Death of Ivan Ilyich*. In his *The Death of Ivan Ilyich and Other Stories*, T. C. B. Cook (trans.). Ware: Wordsworth Classics.

Toynbee, P. 2003. *Hard Work: Life in Low-Pay Britain*. London: Bloomsbury.

Twain, M. [1876] 2006. *The Adventures of Tom Sawyer*. Harmondsworth: Penguin.

Veblen, T. [1899] 1998. *The Theory of the Leisure Class*. Amherst, NY: Prometheus.

Vonnegut, K. 1952. *Player Piano*. New York: Delta.

Waddell, G. & A. K. Burton 2006. *Is Work Good for Your Health and Well-Being?* London: TSO.

Weber, M. [1905] 2002. *The Protestant Ethic and the Spirit of Capitalism*, P. Baehr & G. C. Wells (trans.). Harmondsworth: Penguin.

Whyte, W. H. 1956. *The Organization Man*. New York: Simon & Schuster.

Wilde, O. [1892] 1997. *Lady Windermere's Fan*. In *Collected Works of Oscar Wilde*. Ware: Wordsworth Editions.

Wilde, O. [1891] 2001. *The Soul of Man under Socialism*. In his *The Soul of Man Under Socialism and Selected Critical Prose*. Harmondsworth: Penguin.

Wittgenstein, L. 1998. *Culture and Value*, 2nd rev. edn, P. Winch (trans.). Oxford: Blackwell.

Xenophon. 1994. *Oeconomicus: A Social and Historical Commentary*, S. B. Pomeroy (trans.). Oxford: Oxford University Press.

Young, A. 1771. *The Farmer's Tour through the East of England*, vol. 4. London.

Young, N. (& J. Blackburn) 1979. "Hey Hey, My My (Into the Black)" [Neil Young and Crazy Horse]. On *Rust Never Sleeps* [CD]. © Reprise/Warner Bros. Music Ltd.

Index

Adelman, K. 83
affluence 97–109
Alcidamas 90
alienation 32–8, 78
Allen, W. 126
Amasis 66
Aquinas 19
Arendt, H. 45–6, 117
Aristotle 8, 15–18, 26, 38, 50–53,
    79, 123
Augustine 19
Augustine, N. 83
autonomy 15, 43, 77

Behravesh, N. 116–17
Baron, D. 83
Baudrillard, J. 106
Bauman, Z. 106, 108, 129
Benedict 19
Bentham, J. 80, 119
boredom 30–31, 47, 69, 85,
    119–20, 125
Boyle, R. 5
Bradley, H. 129
Brodsky, J. 125
Bronson, P. 121
Bruckner, P. 124–5
Burton, A. K. 63–4

Calvin, J. 20–23, 25, 47
Camus, A. 29
capitalism 20, 32, 37–8, 40, 59,
    77, 94, 99–100, 113

Carlyle, T. 23–4, 122
Chaplin, C. 75–6, 80
Chesterton, G. K. 70–71
Christo and Jeanne-Claude 55
communism 35–8, 77–8, 94,
    99
consumption 10, 21, 93, 97–
    109, 113, 116, 129
Coward, N. 69
craftsmanship 14–15, 18, 33,
    41–4, 74
Csíkszentmihályi, M. 44

delayed gratification 25, 98–9
Dilenschneider, R. 83
division of labour 32–5, 41–2,
    50, 75, 91
Donkin, R. 129
Dostoyevsky, F. 31
Drucker, P. 84
du Gay, P. 129

Ehrenreich, B. 101
equality of opportunity 54

Ferris, J. 28, 31
Feyerabend, P. 119
flexibility 39–40
Fixx, J. 99
Florida, R. 39
Franklin, B. 22, 71–2, 92
Ford, H. 39, 66, 74–7, 81–2,
    113

fun   10, 68–9, 85

Galbraith, J. K.   98
Gersemann, O.   60
Gini, A.   129
Godbey, G.   61
goods
    external   10, 32, 49–50, 53, 56, 123
    internal   10–11, 49–50, 53, 56, 123
    positional   102
Gorgias   90
Grint, K.   129

happiness   18, 63, 87–8, 95, 123–5
health   57, 62–4, 87
Hegel, G. W. F.   104
Hemsath, D.   85
Herodotus   66
Hesiod   13–14
Himsel, D.   83
Hobbes, T.   69
Hochschild, A. R.   65, 69, 129
Hodgkinson, T.   129
holiday   4, 59, 64, 67, 71
Homer   14
Howell, J.   66
Huxley, A.   52

identity   2, 10–11, 40, 63, 96, 98,
    104–9
idleness   19, 23, 66, 68–9, 92, 96
individualism   25–7, 81

Jackson, P.   56
James, W.   56
job satisfaction   11, 28, 38, 41, 76, 109
Jones, L. B.   83

Kant, I.   30–31, 77, 120
Keynes, J. M.   62, 97
Lawrence Klein, L.   116–17
knowledge workers   8, 79
Krushchev, N.   99

Kubrick, S.   66
Kunde, J.   82

Lafargue, P.   25, 59
leisure   1–2, 6, 8, 16–17, 37–8, 51,
    57–8, 61, 66–72, 97, 122
Lenin, V. I.   77–8
Lindsay, B.   98–9, 129–30
Locke, J.   3
Lovecraft, H. P.   83
Luddites   114–15
Luther, M.   19–21, 47

management   73–86
Mao, T.   55
Marshall, A.   6
Marx, K.   9, 25, 32, 35–8, 41, 77–8,
    94, 100, 104, 112–13
Mayer, G. G.   83
Mayer, T.   83
McJobs   38, 81
meaning   1–3, 25, 27, 29–47, 89, 96,
    106–7, 109, 122–7
Meilaender, G. C.   129
meritocracy   53–4, 95
Mill, J. S.   24–5
money   6–7, 10, 20–21, 87–96
Monty Python   26–7
Morrissey   124
Muirhead, R.   129

Nietzsche, F.   68, 107, 125
Nixon, R.   99–100
Nozick, R.   46

Oates, W. E.   123
Orwell, G.   7–8

Packer, T.   83
Padwa, L.   83
Pepys, S.   123
Pet Shop Boys   99
Peters, T.   84
Plato   15–18, 26, 33, 50–52

poverty 35, 58, 87, 93–4, 100–105
Protestantism 2, 19–23, 25, 47, 98–9, 121
Ptah-Hotep 66

retirement 1–2, 119
Rifkin, J. 112–13, 115
right to work 55–6
Roberts, W. 83
Robinson, J. 61
romanticism 25, 27, 39
Rudnicki, S. 83
Russell, B. 9, 45, 69

Sahlins, M. 58
Schaff, C. 129
Schneider, A. 83
Schor, J. 60–61
self-realization 1–2, 10, 17, 25–6, 32, 36, 39, 49, 56, 82, 104, 107
Sennett, R. 39–40, 99, 130
serfdom 90
Simmel, G. 105
skill 18, 40–43, 74–5, 79, 81–2, 100,
slavery 5, 7, 9, 15–17, 38, 51–3, 58, 90–91, 93
Smith, A. 33–5, 37–8, 41, 90–91, 93–4, 102, 104–6
Socrates 16–17
Spencer, H. 72, 101–2
Stalin, J. 78
standard of living 55, 58, 64, 97, 100
Stein, G. 91
Stewart, P. 7

Taylor, F. W. 72–4, 77–8, 80–82

technology 1, 9, 24, 52, 74–5, 81, 112–15
temporary work 40–41
Tennant, N. 99
The Smiths 124
The The 106
Thomas, K. 129
Tolstoy, L. 124
Toynbee, P. 101
Twain, M. 67–8

unemployment 55, 63–4, 111–17

Veblen, T. 98, 104
vocation 3, 13, 19–21, 25–7, 39
Vonnegut, K. 114

wages 4, 35, 45, 49, 59, 64, 74–6, 87–97, 100–101, 103, 117, 123
minimum 94, 101
Waddell, G. 63–4
Walker, I. 92
Weber, M. 21–2
Weinstein, M. 85
Whitney, J. 83
Whyte, W. H. 26
Wilde, O. 51, 113–14, 127
Wittgenstein, L. 12, 127
workaholic 23, 57, 120, 123–4
working hours 4, 40, 57–67, 78, 115

Xenophon 16–17

Yerkes, L. 85
Young, A. 93
Young, N. 57